AMERICA

AMERICA

AN ANTHOLOGY OF FRANCE AND THE UNITED STATES

Edited by
François Busnel

Black Cat
New York

This work received support from the French Ministry of Foreign Affairs and the Cultural Services of the French Embassy in the United States through their publishing assistance program.

FIRST EDITION

Published simultaneously in Canada
Printed in Canada

This book was designed by Norman E. Tuttle of Alpha Design & Composition

This book is set in 11-pt. ITC New Baskerville by Alpha Design & Composition of Pittsfield, NH

First Grove Atlantic paperback edition: September 2020

Library of Congress Cataloging-in-Publication data is available for this title.

ISBN 978-0-8021-4934-3
eISBN 978-0-8021-4935-0

Black Cat
an imprint of Grove Atlantic
154 West 14th Street
New York, NY 10011

Distributed by Publishers Group West

groveatlantic.com

20 21 22 23   10 9 8 7 6 5 4 3 2 1

TABLE OF
CONTENTS

INTRODUCTION

By
François Busnel

Translated by
Kate Deimling

How many times have you heard someone say, "In the Trump era, truth is stranger than fiction"? This is why some friends and I founded a magazine in which specialists in fiction—novelists—can describe the reality of America.

America came about after Donald Trump was elected. The idea was to tell the story of the world's number one superpower on a quarterly basis, for the length of a presidential term. Trump's victory didn't just stun many Americans. It shook the whole world. As a Frenchman, I feel I belong to what is sometimes called, without irony or submissiveness, the fifty-first state. In other words, the rest of the world. Whether we like it or not, we are all deeply affected by what happens in the United States. If we accept the prevailing cynicism and see Donald Trump simply as a clown, we're just fooling ourselves. The current resident of the White House is much more astute than people think. He shrewdly proves the Mark Twain maxim "All you need in this life is ignorance and confidence; then success is sure."

Since America is anything but homogeneous, *America* has sent writers all over the country, to big cities and little towns, to collect impressions and opinions face-to-face in unbiased fashion, so that literature can cast its net to capture the images that are the truest, the strongest, and sometimes the most disturbing.

Novelists' inspired visions, which are the basis of our approach, seem to be more necessary than ever. We are currently experiencing one of the biggest challenges to democracy: in a puzzling paradox, it seems the more we know about our world—with the Internet, new technologies, and the accessibility of the written word—the less we know what to think about it. There is only one solution: novels. When the authorities preach, novelists take a skeptical stance. When experts try to simplify things, novelists restore complexity. When politicians spin the facts, novelists pull back the curtain on deception. How? By asking questions. By telling stories. How did Trump's reign happen? How did the populist wave triumph, with its accompanying intolerance, ignorance, racism, and partisanship? How are Americans living today, both those who brought this movement to power and those who are simply enduring it? What does the United States of America look like today, after four years of a reign marked by huge political turmoil, threats of war, a surge in protests fighting for racial justice, and the worst public health crisis the country has faced in the last century? A line from investigative journalist Carole Cadwalladr has inspired my readings and travels for years now: "You may know the facts, but you don't know the story." Like many people, I'm a collector of stories.

Novelists don't affirm anything; they seek. Their job is not to solve problems, but to express them. It's quite possible that human stupidity comes simply from trying to have an answer for everything. The novel's wisdom is to have a question for everything. *America* wants to take up this challenge: to understand rather than to judge.

LOS ANGELES

By
Alain Mabanckou

Translated by
Helen Stevenson

ear Marc-Antoine,

Thank you for your e-mail, from which I learned that you spent three days in Los Angeles and were disappointed to discover it was actually just a heap of miserable skyscrapers and towers held hostage by giant motorways. To illustrate the full scope of your resentment, you even say that in the center of town some drivers were so concerned to see you walking, they'd slow down, draw up alongside you, and ask with a kindly air:

"Are you okay, sir? How can I help you?"

You also claim that the City of Angels, which features in the dreams of every global tourist, is ultimately no more than a showcase for extravagance and ostentation, its lethargic inhabitants lounging by the ocean with a glass of mint lemonade. I have to tell you I burst out laughing at this point, because I'm always looking for these people, and it's starting to feel like they only ever appear to lucky travelers like yourself! Also, this caricature of a Californian reminded me of when I lived in France and spent my whole time in the streets trying to find the famous "average Frenchman" with his baguette, Basque beret—and maybe a bottle of red wine and an overripe Camembert . . .

Continuing in the same vein, you tell me that in Venice Beach, where you've rented a small studio, you were appalled to find canals and an artificial lagoon—a "hideous" stage set, a feeble imitation of the real Italian city built on wooden stakes, with its four hundred bridges, a far cry from the vulgar reproductions that obsess Americans and expose their lack of taste and culture, further demonstrated by the replicas of European monuments in Las Vegas.

You conclude by wondering how a cultured man like myself can bear to live in such a place, having experienced both the festive clamor of African capitals and the architectural splendors of the old European cities which, unlike Los Angeles, have their own real history, genuine traditions and unique character . . .

To come straight to the point, my dear Marc-Antoine, I have to say I do not share your view, but I'm sure you are not one of those travelers who, after a very brief stay in a place, consider it "done," and set themselves up as intransigent specialists, to the point of even churning out one of those bestsellers, stuffed with superficial insights and Épinal print–style clichés, that seem to afflict all great American cities. My worry—to be quite frank with you— is that the meager memories you took home with you to Lyons will become your abiding image of Los Angeles and its surrounding area. It's this concern that has moved me to come up with a loose description of where I live, a few unusual places that I love and that fascinate me, those small treasures, you might say, that contribute to my delight and joy in living in California. Delight can also have its dark side, as I know too well, which is why at the end of this letter I will also share with you some of my concerns as a Californian in the wake of the election of Donald J. Trump as president of the United States.

Santa Monica, outpost of Pointe-Noire

As you know, I have lived in Santa Monica, a coastal city on the west side of the county of Los Angeles, for over ten years. With each passing year I have felt an increased sense of belonging, that the city is stretching out its long arms affectionately toward me, and I am drawn to it as I am to Pointe-Noire and Paris. Santa Monica has not just one soul, but many. I need only close my eyes to sense the breath of its first inhabitants—Native Americans of the Tongva tribe—and to hear the distant tread of the Spaniards who made landfall here in the eighteenth century, occupying the exact neighborhood where I live, close to Wilshire Boulevard.

Not a day passes without my sensing the shadow of the Spanish explorer and colonizer Gaspar de Portolá in the features of an old tree, the dead leaves of which, lying at its feet, embody the suffering of those indigenous people whose descendants today are practically strangers in the land of their ancestors. Santa Monica—such a pretty name, a sweet name, derives from Monica of Hippo, a Berber woman, whose saintliness was recognized by both Roman Catholic and Orthodox churches. She was the mother of Saint Augustine, who himself—if I can say this without trampling on the certainties of historians—was an African, since he was born in what at that time was called "the province of Africa," which covered present-day Tunisia and a few parts of Libya and Egypt.

As you will have noted, dear Marc-Antoine, when in Santa Monica I almost feel I'm in Africa, which helps attenuate the pangs of nostalgia that commonly assail the long-term migrant. I am deeply affected by the setting, history, and customs of any place where I might decide to settle for an indeterminate length of time. Had you visited Santa Monica while you were here, you would have observed that the town occupies a central position in Los Angeles county, by which I mean that it is bordered by the most beautiful districts, such as Pacific Palisades, Brentwood, Sawtelle, Mar Vista, and Venice. I feel a deep sense of spiritual connection to these places and to their various cultures, and

Santa Monica Bay offers me freedom of movement and access to the famous Route 66, which used to connect East and West. But rest assured, my friend, I'm not going to give you a history lesson on this mythical stretch of road, since my plan here is to let you into my little secrets concerning Los Angeles and the surrounding area . . .

Where's the center? Where's the periphery?

I will always deeply regret that our paths didn't cross.

We'd have visited the different parts of Mid-Wilshire, between Hollywood and "Downtown" Los Angeles, where you would have noted that it's here, out of the whole county, that the population is most diverse, balanced in such a way that none of the communities concerned—Latinos, African Americans, Asians, and Caucasians—could claim to be dominant. There'd have been lots to do and see in Wilshire Vista, which, before it became "ethnically" diverse, was the African American district. Close by we'd have found the historic and very wealthy district of Windsor Square, where the mayor of Los Angeles resides. A third of the population of Windsor Square was born outside of the United States, and over half come from Asia—in fact, the Koreatown district, on the east side, is one of the most densely populated. Also in Mid-Wilshire is Miracle Mile, a sort of subdistrict within Koreatown, between Wilshire Boulevard and Fairfax and La Brea Avenues, where I would have been thrilled to show you LACMA (Los Angeles County Museum of Art), visited by over a million people every year. This cultural center doesn't just showcase the past: it shows films and regularly holds big concerts, creating monster road blockages, next to which the traffic on Highway 405 would seem like child's play to you. Just beyond the museum, you come to the "Champs-Élysées of America," where I sometimes do a bit of shopping to keep myself "up-to-date" in the clothes department, as the SAPEURS, the Congolese Society of Elegant Dressers, would say . . .

Why my insistence on visiting Mid-Wilshire? So you could see Los Angeles as a vast ensemble and realize that the center of town—or "Downtown," as they say here—is in fact just a space captured in the broad net of a conglomerate of districts, and that it's wrong to expect, as most tourists do, to find a clear divide between a main town on the one hand and a set of dependent—and therefore less important—suburbs on the other. This is the thing I like most about Los Angeles county: you can't tell where the center is, you think you're in and at the center wherever you happen to be. Anyone who lives in Santa Monica or Venice is likely to say "I live in Los Angeles," not by way of abbreviation, but to indicate that the various different towns, the different districts of the county, are all guardians of the spirit of Los Angeles, so that it isn't just a single fixed place, with precise geographical coordinates. The defining characteristic of this metropolis is its ability to exist in all its many different cultures, populations, activities, customs, and even obsessions . . .

Ethiopia in Los Angeles

No doubt you would have asked me where to find Africa in Los Angeles. And I'd have replied that Africa can be found even here in Mid-Wilshire, where I'd have invited you to lunch in Little Ethiopia. We'd have gone down Fairfax Avenue to get to the heart of the place, between Olympic and Pico Boulevards, streets all lined, like Miracle Mile, with shops and restaurants, but here heaped all in a great muddle redeemed only by the festive vibe, swarming with people, in an atmosphere that makes you feel you must be somewhere on the Black Continent. Little Ethiopia started expanding in the early 1990s, gradually replacing the Jewish shopkeepers and, in the 2000s, thanks to the Democratic mayor, James K. Hahn, and in recognition of the concentration of people from the Horn of Africa, the area was officially rebaptized Little Ethiopia.

You'd no doubt have objected that most of the restaurants in this district are Ethiopian or Eritrean and don't represent the cuisine of my continent. You'd not be wrong there, but having said that, Ethiopia is one of the nations we Africans are most proud of. In each of the restaurants in Little Ethiopia—Messob, for example, an Ethiopian restaurant I eat at once a week—you of course encounter the portrait of Haile Selassie I, the last emperor of Ethiopia, considered by the Rastafarian movement to be the leader of the Earth. His heroism is celebrated in the black and white photos and paintings proudly displayed by the owner of Messob. As soon as he sets eyes on me, he's brimming with kindness, patting his little belly before folding me in his arms and exclaiming for joy:

"My brother from Congo-Brazza! Welcome to your home!"

Then, as usual, he'd have told me how Haile Selassie refused to acknowledge Italian colonization, convinced that he alone, as noble representative of the dynasty of Kings David and Solomon, had dominion over his territory.

In this restaurant, Ethiopian music is constantly playing in the background, and sometimes you hear the voice of Bob Marley, global ambassador of rastas. I'd order my usual dish, kitfo, which I love for its spicy flavors of minced beef and homemade cheese, all served with a kind of very thin pancake, called *injera*. The boss would have stood there watching over my first mouthfuls, waiting for my verdict on his cooking. I'd have nodded my head and he'd have whispered, delightedly:

"You should thank King Haile Selassie and Bob Marley . . ."

And once again the owner of Messob Ethiopian restaurant would have gone into great detail, describing the mythical journey the king made to Jamaica, where the whole population was in a state of trance because at last, after so many centuries, the long-awaited Messiah had come!

A bridge for suicide?

After a copious lunch at Messob, we'd have crossed to Pasadena, on the east side of Los Angeles, not to contemplate the splendid San Gabriel Mountains but to admire the Colorado Street Bridge, known as Suicide Bridge. I'd have noticed concern on your face at the dark and daunting name of the structure. Especially as I'd have told you that Suicide Bridge is a fount of different beliefs, legends, and superstitions— as in my country of origin, where bridges are inhabited by wicked spirits who, believing the bridge will collapse and they will drown, are unable to cross the water to find peace in the world beyond. Which is why they cling to the pylons and suspension cables, waiting for the day when the Lord will have mercy on them and suggest an alternative means of transport for getting, at long last, to heaven.

No, I wouldn't have spent too much time scaring you with my African beliefs about bridges. I would simply have informed you that Suicide Bridge, erected at the beginning of the twentieth century, cost the American taxpayer over four million dollars and today is one of the most highly prized of all historic monuments. I'd have gone on at once to tell you that the first time, it was pure chance that brought me face-to-face with this structure.

Chance? Let's say coincidence, rather, as you will soon realize, if you will permit the following digression . . .

When I moved to Santa Monica in 2005, I often used to hang out on Montana Avenue, making my way down to

Ocean Avenue, a stone's throw from the sea, where the famous Santa Monica Pier Ferris wheel, constructed in 1909, dominates the view, towering over the crowd of tourists farther down, at the far end of the jetty. Montana Avenue is pretty much the chic center of the district, with its luxury boutiques, café terraces, and a profusion of convertible cars of varying degrees of fabulousness. It's also the refuge of those movie stars who reject the bright lights of Beverly Hills or Hollywood in favor of the more laid-back feel of Santa Monica and its proximity to the sea.

It was during one of these meanderings, shortly after I had arrived, that I discovered the Aero Theatre cinema—established in the 1930s by the Douglas Aircraft Company—which specializes in showing films around the clock, seven days a week. There's always someone chatty in the box office who'll tell you Robert Redford used to come here when he was a kid.

Though it closed down in 2003 for financial reasons, Aero Theatre opened its doors again the year I came to live in this neighborhood, after complete refurbishment, and instantly became one of those cultural venues the municipality of Santa Monica loves to show off in television ads or leaflets aimed at every resident. It was in this pleasantly intimate establishment that I rediscovered Charlie Chaplin's *The Kid*, and was introduced for the first time to the Suicide Bridge of Pasadena in the scene in which "the Tramp," played by Chaplin himself, comes to the rescue of a young woman accompanied by her child, who is just about to jump to her death from the bridge. *The Kid* came out in 1921, and it was proof that cinema sometimes echoes reality: Suicide Bridge was in fact where many Americans ended their lives when faced with the hardships of the economic crisis of the 1930s. Today, as a precaution, there are barriers to stop visitors from following in the footsteps of these unhappy souls, the most famous of which was the British-American actor, presenter, and model Sam Sarpong, who died in 2015 at age forty. Despite the efforts of his family and the Los Angeles fire department to dissuade him from committing the irrevocable, he threw himself off Suicide Bridge and into the void. Followers of certain television series had enjoyed his appearances on *Bones* and *24*, and in the year of his death, he had been cast in *American Crime Story*. Which is where I bring this digression to a close . . .

A haunted house?

Saddened by our visit to Suicide Bridge, you might have wondered if all our outings would share the same sinister atmosphere. I'd have smiled, thinking you might rather have gone to gaze at the sumptuous buildings of Beverly Hills. Quite understandably—it's what everyone does when they first set foot in Los Angeles. Personally, I hate that kind of outing: you might as well read celebrity magazines; at least they're more informative.

No, we wouldn't have gone looking for such and such an actor's house. We'd have gone to the "Witch's House" (or Spadena House), at 516 North Walden Drive, in Beverly Hills. More shivers down the spine? No, let's just say I'm fascinated by this house, which was originally built in Culver City in 1921 by the film director Harry Oliver, then transferred to Beverly Hills in 1934. Its irregular architecture —the wooden frame with misshapen windows, the gardens stocked with gnarled trees, the bridge (another bridge!) crossing over a ditch—all offer the visitor a unique experience, along with the feeling of being a character in a book of fairy stories, as when the house was still in Culver City and used as a setting for silent movies. Today it is a private residence that can be rented for short leases, and many Californians still believe it was built by one of the seven dwarves from *Snow White*, or that one of its former occupants reappears at Halloween dressed as a witch, handing out sweets to children . . .

I'd have understood if, after visiting these "scary" locations, you'd felt the need to relax in the evening and immerse yourself in the night scene to see how Californians party. We'd have gone to the Circle Bar on Main Street, in Santa Monica, a short distance from Venice. This bar-cum-discotheque, which dates back to the 1940s, is considered one of the trendiest on the west side of Los Angeles. There you'd have met young people from every corner of the States, hoping to be spotted by people in the business. Customers cluster around the centerpiece of the interior, an oval-shaped bar, discussing ideas for stories or adaptations, or simply hanging out in the hope of glimpsing some celebrity, before launching onto the crowded dance floor. What with the old photos on the walls and glaring lights, you'd have been astonished to learn that Jim Morrison and Truman Capote were regulars here . . .

A real writer?

I mention the Circle Bar because I have special memories of it, and whenever I go back there, I am reminded of an experience I had a few years ago that was rather odd, to say the least. I think it might make you smile—at least I hope it will.

Back then, I had a female novelist friend who was writing a book set in Los Angeles. She was spending ten days or so in town, and I have to tell you she did not stop for one minute; she wanted to see everything, do everything, photograph everything, to gather as much material as possible and get all her facts exactly right. She didn't have a driver's license, so she took the bus, walked for miles, got lost, called me for help, and often I'd discover her in districts that were completely new to me. She had, to put it mildly, a loathing of discotheques, because you had to dance, and she was paralyzed at the thought of dancing. I'd had quite a job persuading her to come with me to the

Circle Bar, and as soon as we stepped inside she took up her seat at the bar, firmly planted on her high stool, giving off the message to any potential suitor that no way was she cutting through the crowd to go and make a fool of herself on the dance floor.

She had warned me in advance:

"If anyone asks me to dance, I will deliberately tread on their toes, and it will be their own fault!"

I didn't insist. I was on the dance floor, executing the trickiest steps of the ndombolo, the dance of the two Congos, while some people must have been wondering what planet I was from, with my choreography so out of step with most of the other revelers'.

I was concentrating so hard on what I was doing, I lost sight of my novelist friend. I was starting to get worried, when I caught sight of her, surrounded by four young men with biceps that had clearly been blown way out of proportion in the gym. They wore tight T-shirts and were talking to her about screenplays for feature films and television series she might write, which they'd hand on to the greatest film directors in Hollywood.

I was familiar with this kind of pickup line and had advised my friend to take care, not pay too much attention, and avoid being seduced by empty promises. Alas, she was more than a little receptive, and there was a definite spark between her and the four unknown young men.

By the time I suggested we go on somewhere else in the hope of detaching her from the group, it was one in the morning.

"What? You must be kidding! It's only one in the morning, the bar shuts at two!"

To my utter amazement, she had dashed onto the dance floor and was cutting some moves to the applause of her four admirers.

By now I was feeling pretty impatient and irritated. I left the Circle Bar and went home. Somewhere around three in the morning, I heard a knock on the door. The four Californians were there, with my friend and another woman. The noise level was close to a nocturnal disturbance of the peace, so I decided to shoo the untimely visitors away.

Though at first they resisted, once I threatened to call the forces of law and order, they cleared off, along with the unknown woman. An hour later, my friend told me that the group had taken her overcoat, which she had bought in Germany.

"You know, I really love that coat," she said. "It cost me my ass. I mean, I just can't lose it! I've got the phone number of the girl who was with us, I'll call her, please, can we go and get my coat?"

So the next morning, having received a text from the unknown woman giving the address where the group lived, we set out for Pacific Palisades, a quarter of an hour from Santa Monica. The block was quite high up in the hills, the house itself a very modern building with a glass façade, set in a huge park. The doors were wide open, and the whole place was bathed in silence, which we found quite unsettling, especially as there were signs on the grounds that a struggle had taken place. The trunk of the car was half open, which I didn't find very reassuring, having seen enough films in which dead bodies were hidden in trunks.

We crept up toward the vehicle. The overcoat was there, hooked over the driver's seat. We grabbed it quickly, ran back to my car, and shot off, waiting until we were safely away before bursting into peals of laughter. Since that day, I have not heard a whisper of those so-called "producers," not to mention the young woman they had with them . . .

California, still Democratic . . .

My dear Marc-Antoine, this city of mine, Los Angeles, is a mosaic of little stories like this. I could go on forever. I still haven't written an "American novel," though my

French publisher would like me to. Maybe I never will. Because the freedom I enjoy here brings me more peace of mind than inspiration. But I also find it increasingly stifling, which comes from the political atmosphere in the country as a whole. I've lived through the presidencies of George W. Bush and Barack Obama, each of whom occupied the White House for two successive terms before Donald Trump came to power. I could just have rejoiced in the privilege of living in California, a state that votes overwhelmingly for the Democratic Party in the primaries: over 60 percent for Hillary Clinton in the 2016 election, with a peak of 85 percent in a city like San Francisco . . . So I completely understand that some Californians, recognizing the danger of an America folded in on itself, as envisaged by the current powers that be, favor a veritable "Calexit." But, my dear friend, I am keeping my head here, because it would be easier to pass an elephant through the eye of a needle than to obtain independence for California. In the absence of such a step, we are witnessing a wave of protests in Los Angeles, but also in most large cities in the country, particularly in Chicago and New York, with the motto "Not My President." And the presidential decree on immigration is seen here as a backward step and a denial of the tradition of hospitality that is special to Los Angeles, the whole of California, and indeed a nation that rose to greatness thanks to the support of migrants.

For my own part, I need hardly say that my door will always be open to you, and that next time we really must make sure we're in tune, so we don't miss one another again.

Till we meet, then, and with good wishes,
A.

FROM
CHICAGO
TO
NEW ORLEANS

By
Philippe Besson

Translated by
Sandra Smith

don't exactly know which of us had the idea. But I think that it was S. who first said: "We could travel across America by car." I believe he was thinking of taking Route 66, which runs from Chicago to Santa Monica. Romantic pipe dreams seem to last forever.

I objected at once (I am undoubtedly not romantic enough, or quite simply I've gotten too old): "You have no idea how exhausting that would be; let's find a shorter route." But I do remember that I liked the idea of starting in Illinois.

Chicago: my first encounter with the United States. That was twenty-five years ago. I'd gone to visit a French friend who had settled down there, doing odd jobs to earn a living and hoping one day to work in the movies (he should have chosen LA, and even in LA, his chances would have been minuscule). He lived in a tiny apartment in the Loop, next to an elevated subway line. His windows shook when the train went by. The screeching of the wheels was shrill to my ears. Those first few days, it took me hours to fall asleep, despite the jet lag. And what's more, the city was having a horrible heat wave. The temperature was over one hundred degrees every day. On television, they even went so far as asking people not to use their ovens. That shocked me.

In short, I thought it would be good to go back there for the first time in a quarter of a century. Even if it's always a little strange to confront your memories with reality. Dangerous too.

Suddenly I remember: S. came back with: "In that case, let's drive from north to south, starting from the Midwest and finishing in the Deep South." "Agreed," I said. Without hesitating. Without thinking about it. Here we go.

But first, we had to get into the country. That meant an eight-hour flight and getting through border security at the airport. S. and I went up together to the official, a poker-faced young man who immediately looked at us suspiciously for a long time. I want to believe that neither our sexual orientation (presumed) nor the age difference between us (obvious) was the cause of that look; that it was, in fact, simply an occupational hazard. But then, the verdict was delivered: I was allowed into the United States with no more red tape. But S. was instructed to report to the Immigration Office for questioning. It was pointless to ask why this difference in our treatment: S. has a last name that sounds Arabic, I don't. I muse on the fact that the terrorists have won. They have transformed some people into suspects and made others suspicious. At Immigration and Customs, all you need to do is look at the people waiting to go through in-depth interrogation to confirm this: they all look more or less alike.

One hour and a dose of humiliation later, we climb into a taxi. During the ride, images from my first stay come back to me. The first one is a memory from the banks of Lake Michigan: a lake so vast that I thought I was at the edge of the sea as I basked on the beach. And when I turned around to look behind me, I saw a row of tall, elegant buildings. I also remember, but less clearly, Grant Park: its green grass, so very green that it looked almost artificial, especially under the burning, harsh sunlight.

But reality puts an end to my daydreams: on the radio, they are talking about Donald Trump, who is celebrating his first six months in the White House. Celebrating is, in fact, quite a grand word, since almost everyone watching him agrees that his track record is extraordinarily limited.

Not a single law voted on. Decrees rejected. International agreements condemned. Backtracking, disappointments, defeats. A low popularity rate. He alone bellows out improbable victories through tweets that become more and more surreal—nearly a thousand of them since he took office! The driver, who is surreptitiously looking at us in his rearview mirror, calls out: "He cracks me up; what do you think?" We smile without replying, not sure we can tell which side he's leaning toward and too tired to get into a political debate.

We also know that the outrageous White House Press Secretary, Sean Spicer, has just resigned. He must no longer have gotten away with saying everything and then the opposite, giving opinions while being sure of nothing, being refuted after having been encouraged, defending the indefensible, relentlessly attacking journalists, the very same people who sat opposite him in the press briefing room. We're almost relieved for him.

We drop our bags off at an apartment we've rented in the River North neighborhood, at the intersection of Orleans Street and Oak Street, before heading out almost immediately to take in the city. One look and I can see that it has changed since I was young: more skyscrapers have sprung up; architectural innovations have produced a few spectacular examples, some fantastic, some quirky, with rooftop gardens just about everywhere, former factories now housing lofts. In short, I have (undoubtedly) aged, and Chicago has rejuvenated.

I also notice that the police presence has heightened to bring back a sense of security that had lapsed for a while. In the past, crime movies were filmed here: now, it's mainly romantic comedies or science fiction movies because, in both cases, the setting is appropriate.

The Sears Tower has been renamed: it's now called the Willis Tower and can no longer proudly proclaim to be the tallest building in America. As for Grant Park, it now connects with Millennium Park, which houses contemporary works of art, such as the famous *Cloud Gate*, an enormous, mirror-like sculpture made of stainless steel, designed by Anish Kapoor, that looks more like a giant bean than the door to the clouds that I imagined.

Nevertheless, Chicago has not changed completely from top to bottom: it remains the vibrant, cosmopolitan city I once knew. The multicultural neighborhoods are still there, the subway lines still produce a formidable racket above our heads along the rusty metal tracks, and the license plates on the cars continue to remind us that this is truly "the Land of Lincoln." Culture is visible everywhere, including on the backs of buses, where I am surprised to find an ad for the real estate company domu.com, along with a quote from Sarah Bernhardt, who toured here in 1905 and 1912, that reads: "I adore Chicago. It is the pulse of America."

A little to the north, in Boystown, about one hundred yards from the lake, the atmosphere is always picturesque and the night life wild. This is where the gay community has been gathering for more than thirty years. It's impossible to miss it: the rainbow-colored columns show the way for any lost sheep. At the Sidetrack Bar, young men sometimes lose their virginity and find their identity in one night. In conservative America, steeped in religion, where family is more important than anything, this brazen oasis is considered something of a miracle, and holding our drinks, we weave our way through it. At Replay, Chris, an athletic thirty-something, confirms this: "The victory of that asshole Trump hasn't changed a thing: we're having a good time here, just like before. People haven't changed the way they see us. And if they started to look at us sideways, we'd tell them to go fuck themselves!" And he raises his middle finger, laughing, while Gloria Gaynor belts out "I Will Survive." It's true: who would have believed that Trump would one day win that damn election?

We stayed in the area for a few days, intoxicated by its vitality, soaking in its creativity, yet knowing perfectly well that the next part of our journey would probably be very different. In short, we were gathering the strength we would need to head into battle.

One morning, after picking up a rental car, we headed out to Cincinnati, our next stop, but first we had to cross Indiana. To me, Indiana is first and foremost the state where James Dean was born. I love that wild, inconsolable, and amazing young man so much that I wrote a book about him. To do that, at the time, I surveyed the places he had lived—Santa Monica with its palm trees, Hollywood with its illusions, the sidewalks of New York, and even Cholame, California, where he died while driving to Salinas—but I had never been to Indiana. So I had to imagine the terrible winters and unbearable summers in Marion, the town where he was born, had to imagine him as a child playing in the snow or running until he was out of breath in the fields scorched by the sun. I had imagined that it was a difficult, harsh place. Today, I see it for myself. Corn growing as far as the eye can see, haystacks by the dozens, hills full of greenery, a few wind turbines to break the monotony. Sometimes you don't see a single house for miles, and when you finally do, it is almost always flying an American flag. You have to like silence, solitude, God, and country to live here. Some faces are craggy, prematurely old. The people from here are nicknamed *Hoosiers*, which means hillbillies or rednecks. (But they're the ones who gave America its new vice president. Mike Pence was the governor of this state: "a Christian, a conservative, and a Republican, in that order," is how he describes himself. And the way things are going, he probably won't stay content with the vice presidency.)

As I was saying, I hadn't visited Fairmount, where Jimmy grew up, and where he's buried. This time, the temptation was too great: we would make a detour. The town honors its idol in its own way, with a sign, a statue, and a "historical museum," a somewhat pompous name for the small building with red walls we visited. Two delightful old ladies with white hair eagerly greet us there—we're the first visitors of the day. The older one murmurs: "You've come because you love Jimmy, correct?" Correct. She immediately gives us a guided tour. A few personal effects of the town's famous child are displayed in glass cases: baby clothing, hand-written notes, drawings, letters, props from his movies. This somewhat laughable exhibit ends up being sublime and deeply moving.

Next, at the intersection of Adams and Vine, we look for the old school of the little genius, but we find nothing but a pile of rubble. The school no longer exists; it has just been demolished. Fans sometimes come to steal a brick, as a kind of lucky charm. S., who notices my disappointment, tries to make a joke: "It's like the song by Isabelle Adjani: 'you're in a state near Ohio, you're feelin' low.'"

We finally head to the cemetery. It is vast, but nothing points to the grave, which is minuscule: a simple stone set on the grass next to a gravel walkway, alongside so many others, unimpressive, with two dates, the year of his birth and of his death. A few small pebbles placed on the top of the stone as an offering to the deceased, a faded bouquet of flowers, some potted plants. That's all. We leave. My heart is aching.

As we approach Ohio, my thoughts slowly drift back to politics. I think about the fact that this is one of the famous swing states that gave Trump victory. In 2008 and 2012, Obama won it easily. But in 2016, the majority of the state went to the billionaire: the Republican candidate beat Hillary Clinton by nine points. He was dominant throughout the entire state, except in the three main cities: Cleveland, Columbus, and Cincinnati. The reasons for this about-face have been explained at length: this is the Rust Belt, the industrial region that was bled dry by the economic crisis and where people are finding it difficult to change jobs.

The outcasts from the steel industry and coal mines naturally turned to the person who claimed he could save them. The farmers are also having trouble making ends meet and are repelled by the elites who don't care about their fate: Hillary was a turn-off to them.

And, contrary to what we might think, enthusiasm for Trump has not waned. In Bridgetown, on the I-74, where we stopped for coffee, Michael, a forty-five-year-old long-standing Democrat, attracted by our French accents to the point of starting up a conversation, confirmed this: Trump is still appealing here. He tells us that in Youngstown, in the north of the state, a city that symbolizes the blue-collar working-class community almost to the point of caricature, twenty thousand people have just given a triumphant welcome to the president. Ordinary people, who call themselves patriots, who do not understand the stubbornness that rules their hero, who continue to find him different, "refreshing," who still believe in the myth of "the true America that is suffering from the arrogance of Washington." "These people exist, and they haven't changed their minds," Michael laments. "And yet, they will be the principal victims of Trumpism. Look at what is happening to Obamacare. If the Republicans manage to do away with it, these people will be very vulnerable." I point out to him that that latest attempt to repeal it failed again a few days before. "They'll try again. Trump is the kind of person who never gives in. And he isn't interested in reality."

It's a return to reality, in fact, as we enter Cincinnati. We immediately realize we are in a close-knit community, where the black population is very large—nearly one resident out of two, according to official statistics. If it was pioneer country in the past, with time it has become more unassuming while remaining a home for immigrants and a center of industry. It prides itself on its impressive suspension bridge (not advisable for people who get vertigo, like me), and Fountain Square lies at the heart of the city.

Not very far away, on the corner of Fifth and Walnut Street, there are a handful of people waving signs that say "Black Lives Matter." A young woman who notices my curiosity comes over and asks me whether I "support them." I ask her to explain. So Melissa tells me about Samuel DuBose, a forty-three-year-old black man, killed two years ago by Ray Tensing, a twenty-five-year-old white police officer, when he stopped DuBose's car. Tensing pulled out his gun and fired at close range because DuBose looked like he was about to drive off. DuBose was unarmed, and the cop normally wore a T-shirt with the Confederate flag on it under his uniform. The officer immediately pleaded self-defense, except that the video footage taken from the bodycam he was wearing radically contradicted his version of events. The first trial that took place resulted in a hung jury. A second trial ended in May 2017 with the same result, so the prosecutor has just decided to drop the case against the officer. "And so," Melissa tells me, "you can kill black people with impunity in this city, in this country, risking nothing! We're here to say that this is unacceptable." Fewer than a dozen people are demonstrating. Melissa is preaching in a desert. Racism still has many happy days ahead. It remains the tragic failure of the Obama era.

Otherwise, life seems rather peaceful in this place. Happy, too, sometimes. The Below Zero Lounge sells blue and green cocktails, and when evening comes, drag shows feature performers with names like Mystique Summers or Divine Cher. S. and I sing karaoke, trying to perform "Finally" by CeCe Peniston, which turns out to be impossible. We are applauded for our "charming accents," an elegant way of making us understand that our nationality is obvious and that karaoke is not for us.

Two days later, we're back on the road heading to Kentucky, to the west of the Appalachians, the state that marks the boundary between the North and South. It is especially famous for being the birthplace of American whiskey.

On the radio, they are reporting the firing of the White House Director of Communications, the blaringly noisy Anthony Scaramucci, who had only been appointed ten days before. Ten days during which he had gotten the president's chief of staff to resign and spoken with such dirty language that certain newspapers didn't think they should quote him. (I have no such inhibitions: he said, "fucking paranoid" and "suck my dick.") The general consensus is that chaos reigns in the White House. There is a blazing sun.

We stop in Carroll County. No one here is interested in the madness in Washington. Here, the subject of conversation is Jesus Chavez, fifty-six, a small business owner who runs a maintenance company. Chavez refused to pay a plumber he had just hired for a small contract, threatening to report him to the Department of Immigration on the grounds that he might be an illegal immigrant. The plumber went to the police and reported the blackmail. Chavez was arrested and put in prison for human trafficking. In brief, the worst of capitalism and the best of racism joined together in a single act, although some people seem to think that Chavez wasn't wrong.

We don't hang around. Even more so because a sign at the side of the road proudly proclaims that Kentucky has the greatest number of guns per capita. Frankly not very reassuring.

(Something funny: A little farther along, there is another sign, an ad this time, that catches our attention. An ad for Spotify. Scanning the news and reminding everyone of the Muslim Ban, the musical streaming service found a credo: "When people can't travel, music will." These two different Americas were only ten miles apart. Unless they're actually the same America.)

A priori, Tennessee does not seem much more welcoming than Kentucky, when you remember that the state was one of the principle battlefields of the American Civil War, and that the Ku Klux Klan was born here in 1865, a result of the Confederate defeat. And when you also know that the very conservative Southern Baptist Convention dominates thinking here, and that Trump received 61 percent of the votes in 2016. And when you find out that just a few days before, a judge in White County suggested a deal that was at least unique (and probably unconstitutional) for people in jail in the county: thirty days taken off their jail time if they agree to have a vasectomy (for men) or to go on hormonal contraceptives (for women).

To avoid depression, we're better off remembering that Tennessee is also the birthplace of country, rock, and the blues. And that Memphis, one of the two great cities in the state, is the home of Graceland, where Elvis Presley found eternal rest. And besides, commemorations are in preparation, for the King left this earth exactly forty years ago. Done in by too much alcohol, too many drugs, too much of everything, he ended life bloated, ridiculous, tragic. But here, you don't make jokes about Tennessee's idol. You speak of him with reverence. Warren, in his late sixties, wears worn-out cowboy boots and is having a few pints of beer at the bar. He asserts, with the look of someone who knows for sure but isn't allowed to say how, that Elvis is, "of course" still alive. Elvis spends his days peacefully in some backwater, on a ranch hidden from view. He has long white hair, wears a cowboy hat, and has gotten so thin that people don't recognize him; only a few insiders take their hats off as he walks by, promising to keep his secret. S. says: "This guy is crazy." I reply: "No. He needs to believe it, that's all." And what difference is there, in the end, between people who believe in God and those who are convinced that Elvis isn't dead?

If you're not interested in either rock 'n' roll or keeping life preserved with mothballs, all that is left, here as elsewhere, is baseball and football, two other religions. Every large city we've passed through up till now has had its

two stadiums (generally enormous outdoor ones, financed
by a sponsor), its favorite teams, its mascots, and the games
themselves. The number of season-ticket holders equals the
number of seats. Tickets are bought for the entire season
as soon as they go on sale. In bars, the TVs are automatically tuned to sports channels, and the calendar of games
is posted. One way, like any other, to ward off boredom.
Or to organize your existence.

The car takes off again toward Alabama. I confess a
certain sense of apprehension. First of all, the state remains
a symbol of slavery, and also of segregation. I want to believe
that the past is dead and buried. The state is also located at
the heart of what is known as the Bible Belt, and I am wary
of people who are convinced that God rules over everyone. On the road, there is an enormous sign advertising
a Christian community with a terrifying message: "Where
will you spend eternity: in HEAVEN or HELL? The choice
is yours." But the countryside is absolutely beautiful, with
stony mountains, tree-lined plains, and navigable rivers.

Birmingham, where we stop while muggy rain falls
on the streets, does not, sadly, have the same charm. It is
cradled in a valley where the Appalachian Mountains end
and can certainly pride itself on beautiful gardens and old
theaters, but it still carries the stigma of the white flight of
the 1990s and 2000s due to the decline in industry.

And yet, what seems to concern the population is not
that memory, and even less the memory of Martin Luther
King Jr., who was imprisoned here in 1963 during the civil
rights movement, but the gentrification of the city center.
So much so that the candidates in local elections to be
held at the end of the month are required to respond to a
detailed questionnaire specifically about urban gentrification and to suggest solutions. You have to understand that
in Avondale and Lakeview, hundreds of luxury apartments
have been built in the past few years—and the rents are
now so high that low-income residents are kicked out. The

best schools are located in those areas, businesses that sell expensive, high-end products are flourishing there, and trendy places are opening up. Some people are happy about what they are calling a "renaissance"—that will bring the white people back—while others are worried about this new form of segregation. The mayoral candidates themselves go back and forth between contentment and anxiety. The truth is that this kind of impetus can be difficult to contain. It moves forward as part of history. But a city known for its history of poverty and struggle against the separation of populations that finds itself caught up again in this issue cannot fail to ask questions. It seems the issue of money has replaced the issue of race, and sometimes, the two overlap.

Jill, who is renting us her apartment, talks about it ingenuously in other terms: "You absolutely must go to El Barrio on Second Avenue! It's a bar and restaurant that has a fabulous brunch menu. It's full every night and perfect for hipsters." Even if I definitely do not fall into that category, I assume that she automatically put S. in it, given his strange hat and short pants. We take her advice. We meet very few black people and very few poor people at El Barrio.

The journey continues. It takes us to Mississippi. I've dreamed about Mississippi for a long time. I think a lot of people dream about Mississippi. It undoubtedly has to do with the name. A name that has immense power to evoke memories. Or perhaps because of the books by Mark Twain (we all know them), in which the Mississippi River played such a memorable role. Now, we must test the fantasy against reality. There are things that live up to expectations: the immense forests of live oak, cedar, and pine trees, deep waters, somber and majestic, steel bridges, a few plantation-style residences with white porticos (even if they do evoke a tragic history). And then there are things that disappoint: shopping centers as you enter the cities, the Confederate flags, conservatism, and poverty.

We stop at Laurel, by chance, because we're getting tired. Laurel is almost nothing—just a few calm streets, well-kept lawns, a sports field, a café with no one sitting outside—normal life far from the busy din, life as you sometimes want it to be when, caught up in the whirlwind, you yearn for calm, a slower pace. No, Laurel is nothing, and yet we still find something there: the "light in August"—as Faulkner would put it—on the houses with multicolored facades. And that is priceless.

The journey continues, and we find yet another America. The one, for example, where you get change in the service station shops. The one where you wolf down po'boys at KY's Olde Towne Bicycle Shop in Slidell, on the other side of Lake Pontchartrain, where few tourists have probably ever set foot. There, a father, aged fifty-five, and his son, thirty-five, both wearing green fatigues, meet each other at noon every Saturday, and take off their baseball caps when their order comes so they can say a prayer. (Afterward, what could they talk about? A war that one of them has fought in? One of those wars you wage in the name of a certain idea of Good and Evil?) This America moves around in busted up pickup trucks, on side roads, with a dog in the back whose tongue is hanging out as the hot wind lashes his face. An America concerned about the passing weather or the passing time.

And then we get to New Orleans. I'm happy to be back here, where I've been four or five times. I saw the city before Hurricane Katrina. I saw it after the devastation, still gutted. I saw a city lose its population, a city with "a black majority" turn into a "white majority." I saw houses demolished and houses for sale. Today, the scars of the destruction have disappeared. But what about the memory of the terror? How do you manage to live with the memory of such terror, how? And how do you manage to live with the memory of those who died—nearly two thousand in just a few hours—in this place where people believe in voodoo, in this city that has a Museum of Death?

The city has somehow kept its taste for celebrations, a way to forget, or to bear it. The French Quarter is the best example—or the worst caricature—of this. Here, from early afternoon until late into the night, you see stumbling drunks who look dangerous; and young women in very short mini-skirts that are a little vulgar, who talk loudly while waving around mardi gras necklaces; mediums who cast spells; people who sway to the music and tequila in the stifling heat. At the Corner Pocket, lustful young men dance on the counter, wearing very little clothing, for gentlemen of a certain age who slip money into their white underpants or offer to buy them a drink. In the evening, the streets are full of the smell of pot, and in the early morning, a mixture of vomit and detergent.

A candidate in the upcoming mayoral primary election, bar owner Patrick Van Hoorebeek, even went so far as to adopt the following campaign slogan: "More Wine, Less Crime" (I swear I'm not making this up). Many people use another expression to sum up this state of mind: "Southern decadence."

To make the folklore complete, jazz musicians play on the sidewalks—but in reality, they are playing only for the tourists, for the few dollars thrown into the hats they have in front of them, set down on the shiny cobblestones. And while the streets have the names of French cities—Toulouse, Orleans, Chartres—it's been ages since anyone spoke French here. Maybe just a few older people, in the hope of keeping the myth alive.

And yet, the splendor of the place remains: wrought iron balconies with wisteria tumbling down, the beautiful white church in Jackson Square, the riverboats on the Mississippi, and even a tropical storm, whose rare ferocity makes the headlines of the local newspapers—all these things ensure that the legend will survive.

But we grow tired of everything, including the splendor, and finally, one morning, we bolt, with the goal of getting closer to the Gulf of Mexico. Leaving behind the intertwining ramps of the highway, the outlines of the buildings growing fainter and fainter, we head deeper into the country, where the roads are slower, sometimes in a bad state of repair, often surrounded by water. Cyprus trees emerge from the swamps like creatures that are half alive, half dead. Very few people can be seen. We drive alongside a bayou infested with mosquitos and catch a glimpse of an old man steering a makeshift boat, far from the organized guided tours. Then we go over a wobbly bridge. And we come to the end of dry land, Grand Isle, set on a long stretch of sand, which the Cajuns, descendants of the Acadian settlers, call home. Now, we see nothing in front of us but the ocean.

Our journey has finally come to an end. Another one will surely now begin.

ORANGE IS
THE NEW
BLACK

By
Richard Powers

Waking up each morning to the latest episode of *The Trump Show* is a bit like taking part in one of those early Cold War–era unregulated experiments that induced psychic trauma in unwitting victims in order to study the lasting effects. This morning I awoke to the news that the White House is moving ahead with its plan to destroy the mandate for automotive fuel efficiency enacted by the Obama administration. Since Trump's political thought has long consisted primarily of knee-jerk repudiation of anything accomplished by the world's once-most-powerful black man, that proclamation, in itself, does not surprise me. But the announcement was accompanied by another one that makes a mockery of the core tenet of conservative ideology: Trump's people have also moved to eliminate California's freedom to set a fuel standard that improves upon the national goal.

I blink while finishing my breakfast and read the story again. Even after a year and a half of incredulity, I'm struggling with this one. But yes: I've understood it properly. The leader of the party of States' Rights, the champion for getting Big Government out of regional and local affairs, the man who pardoned ranchers for committing open, armed rebellion against federal overreach is telling California—a state that at this very moment is paying the crippling price of global warming—that Washington forbids it to clean up its air and reduce its carbon footprint. California's cars must become dirtier and less efficient once again. Letting the elected representatives of that state ask for anything better would, Trump insists, be unfair to the American people and American business.

Of course, this latest push to demolish environmental standards by unilaterally imposed executive fiat has little to do with business (which has been profiting nicely from the conversion of its fleets to more efficient models) or with the economy (certainly not the economy of a state that has long paid massive hidden costs in the health and well-being of its people). California now battles constantly for survival against the most deadly and destructive fires in history, fires bred and exacerbated by the global warming that the Trump administration prohibits the state from taking action against. Two dozen of these enormous fires are blazing through the West this very morning. Toxic air from fifteen million Californian cars and multiple runaway wildfires is killing people and shortening lives even as I struggle to absorb this bit of news. But Washington forbids the affected people to address the crisis.

The Clean Air Act was passed half a century ago, with the understanding that each state must at least meet the national mandate for motor vehicle emissions. If any state wanted to do better on its own, the federal government has long declared, then more power to it. Now Trump is reversing that half a century of carefully coordinated, bipartisan protocol. And Republicans everywhere are once more caving to the blatant federal overreach, despite its crippling costs.

This development should by now be old news to me, part of a broader pattern that, even in my daily traumatized state, I have come to understand all too well. Fighting back the weary nausea brought on by the story and hoping to get on with my own day's work, I can't help seeing this attack on the health of Americans as just another small assault in an enormous campaign against the future. Like so much else that our game show president has initiated—his trade wars, his Wall, his attacks on NATO allies, his rolling back of legal protections for the marginalized and disenfranchised —Trump's war on California and his destruction of fifty years of environmental protocol have nothing to do with conservatism or the search for national prosperity. He is simply trying to revive an old idea of exceptionalism and privilege that has been moribund for decades now.

George Lakoff, the University of California, Berkeley, professor of linguistics and cognitive science, has said it best: Trump's political platform is based entirely on the appeal of "stern paternalism," a vision of a bygone world that puts men above women, whites above all other races and ethnicities, America above all other countries, and humans above and against all other living things. Of course Trump hates California, that multiracial, multiethnic, multicultural state that has already committed itself to the world of the future. Of course he hates any mandate that asks Americans to accommodate the health of an atmosphere that we share with the rest of the world. Of course he needs to go on pretending that human enterprise knows no limits and is accountable to nothing.

Henry Ford, the man who put the automobile within reach of the average American consumer, once famously said that the public could have a car painted in any color that it liked, so long as it was black. Trump's daily message to his base may well be precisely this: America can have greatness in any hue that it wants, so long as it is dominant, unilateral, unaccountable, and white.

By afternoon, Trump, the consummate "reality" entertainer, has rolled on to other, more exciting, more outrageous episodes in his never-ending Season One. His war against California's efforts to save itself quickly gets buried under new and novel escapades: Battles with the Koch brothers and other alpha males within his own party.

Tweets ordering his Attorney General to end the investigation into Russian election meddling, collusion, and obstruc-
tion of justice. So it goes, every day, on *The Trump Show*. It
does not matter what the *issues* are, so long as the man in
the White House has all eyes on him.

By evening, shell-shocked and twitching as I fall
asleep, I begin to see that I've gotten the formula slightly
wrong. We, the American audience to this commandeering
of democracy, are allowed to have a country in any color
we want, so long as it's orange.

THE OUTSKIRTS OF
THE CITY

By
Marie Darrieussecq

Translated by
Penny Hueston

was born in Bayonne, in the French Basque Country, so for a long time I daydreamed about going to Bayonne, New Jersey. In March 2019, my daughter and I were staying at a friend's place on the forty-third floor of a tower in Brooklyn; our trip to New York was a present to my daughter for her fifteenth birthday. We were hypnotized by the extraordinary view of the Statue of Liberty and Ellis Island. And every morning, on the other side of the Hudson, a broad, pale smudge lit up beneath the rising sun. Bayonne. I didn't have binoculars, but I could make out a port area, warehouses, silos, and two very big bridges straddling the water like skeletal dinosaurs.

The geography of New York City is complex. The satellite images show landmasses that seem to have been carved out of the sea with a knife. Bayonne is on a peninsula, Manhattan is an island, and Brooklyn is the western tip of Long Island. There are islands everywhere. In some places, a sandy strip runs along the coast, like on Long Beach or on Fire Island. And, directly opposite, on the other shore of the Atlantic, is the other Bayonne.

One evening, Antoine, a friend of a friend, attended a lecture I gave at New York University, and we discovered that we shared a taste for what are known as "non-places," places on the periphery. He had been living in New York for twenty years but had never been to Bayonne—why bother? Using the pretext of a promotional flyer he had received that very morning, he thought it would be amusing to attend the grand opening of an enormous supermarket over there. We were to meet at the Hoboken train station, from where we'd head to Bayonne by car. My daughter raised her eyebrows, but the prospect of seeing Manhattan from the other side—and her kindness in indulging her mother's whims—meant that we set off early and in a good mood.

Hoboken is lucky enough to have the PATH train, which crosses the Hudson in fifteen minutes. The neighboring Jersey City became gentrified through the same public-transport magic and now resembles Brooklyn with its brownstones and its hipster city center. But it takes more than an hour to get from Manhattan to Bayonne. A proposal for a ferry, which would take ten minutes from one side of the river to the other, has been agreed on, and, if all goes to plan, the service could start operating as early as September 2020.

You begin to understand Bayonne when you realize that the Statue of Liberty has its back to the place. You can see only the crown on top of her green copper hair, her face turned toward Manhattan. Bayonne's small city center is made up of pretty streets, neat rows of modestly proportioned, almost identical wooden houses in pastel shades. All of a sudden there's a colorful, sixties, Florida-style building that jars with these East Coast surroundings. The public high school, like a huge gothic mansion, is an impressive sight. The public library is housed in a beautiful colonnaded building that dates back to 1904. And then, at the end of the city's few streets, two colossal bridges sever the space. Light pours forth, the sky is vast, but every walkway is a dead end, cut off by the water. The streets peter out into indeterminate areas, where we drive past gigantic warehouses.

It's very cold. Wire fencing everywhere. No one around. The chemical factories seem deserted, as if they were operating of their own accord, enormous pipes, pumps, winches, nuts and bolts the size of our heads. At the base of some massive spherical silos, a man in overalls, alone, rails against God. Endless oil tanks lined up ad infinitum. Hummocks of gravel and other materials. A strong sulfurous smell lingers, just as in the much smaller port of my birthplace. We can see only a few workers in fluorescent vests on a military frigate in the dry dock. An abandoned mobile home, covered in brambles, strewn with old domestic items, seems to belong in the opening scene of a David Lynch film. Imagine *Twin Peaks* without the mountains or the forest, and with the sea instead, broken up by a military-industrial port. It's as if Bayonne has been breached by a dream fault line that makes strange places accessible.

We pluck up our courage to push open the door of "Starting Point," which, indeed, turns out to be the departure point for this expedition. We have been wandering around for a little while beneath the vast pylons of a metal bridge that is mind-bogglingly high. From the outside, Starting Point is nothing more than a sign on an off-white, windowless shed. Pole dancing, maybe? A brothel for sailors? We enter a friendly restaurant-bar, open in the middle of the afternoon, where overweight families are eating fried food and old men are watching a football match on the TV.

We gather by the bar. A Budweiser in front of him, Francis Murphy is waiting for his washing to finish its cycle in the laundromat next door. He's immediately amused by the fact that I was born in Bayonne, France. This anecdote will be my passport everywhere in the city—if in fact I need one, because everybody is extremely welcoming. "Bayonne ham!" Francis exclaims. "Nice and sweet." He used to be a chef and can't speak highly enough of the ham from *my* Bayonne. In the past he found some in Weehawken, not far from here, in a deli that has since closed down. Francis used to work at the Chart House, an upscale restaurant with a view across to Manhattan. The Chart House burned down. Francis launches into a complicated explanation of electrical fires.

I don't know if Murphy is his real surname, but that's what he's called by his buddy, who is as Irish as he is, and who is laden with green scarves he's selling for St. Patrick's Day. The two friends have red faces and cube-shaped heads and are downing as many Buds as I am Cokes. Francis is around sixty. He had another buddy here, a native of Tromsø. Tromsø, in Norway, is inside the Arctic Circle. "Well, it turns out that it's warmer there than in Bayonne, New Jersey. It can get down to minus ten degrees here," Francis declares, and when I realize he means degrees Fahrenheit, I agree with him: that's really cold, the equivalent of twenty-three below in degrees Celsius. "It's because of our geographical position," he says, "right at the end of the landmass. Because of the sea and the wind. Everything is flat here."

Bayonne, at the very end of the world, and at the very end of the wind. Francis's retired buddies have all left the city to go farther south. "You only need to go as few as a hundred miles down this fucking icy coast to find some warmth," he tells me. Soon, he's going to move to Atlantic City, the casino town. "I want to gamble myself to death!" Francis used to love Bayonne. But the new bridge has changed everything; Francis's world has gone, because the rest of the world has arrived, and Francis seems to blame the bridge for exposing the city to people from everywhere else: "The newcomers," he explains, "haven't got a clue about the spirit of Bayonne. There are a lot of Spanish, and a real lot of people from the Middle East. Not so many Syrians, no, because of the war, but Egyptians, yes. It's changed everything."

"But aren't you all immigrants here?" I ask.

"We're all Irish," he says proudly. "And Italians and Polish as well. And it was the Dutch who founded the city.

And, of course, before that, there were the Indians," he adds, lost in thought now.

We fall silent for a moment. As is often the case when I'm in the United States, I try to imagine the place emptied of concrete and asphalt, populated by nomads and bison.

So it was not the Basque people who founded this city. The name refers only to the idea of a bay, *Bay-On*. In fact, two large bays and a stretch of water surround it: Newark Bay, New York Bay, and the peculiarly named Kill Van Kull, the strait onto which our little bar, Starting Point, would look out, if it had windows. The demographic details from Wikipedia, which I consult in English so I can present them to Francis, reveal that people of Hispanic origin make up 25 percent of the population, that indeed there are quite a number of Egyptians, and that the city is rather youthful, with an average age of thirty-eight in a total population of 62,000. We also discuss the meaning of the surprising municipal flag, which I have seen flying everywhere alongside the American flag: it looks like a French flag with a boat in the middle, except that the colors could be from Holland in former times. In any case, the famous Bayonne Bridge was for many years the longest steel arch bridge in the world, before it was superseded by four other bridges. It connects New Jersey with Staten Island and, from there, New York.

New York? Francis never goes there anymore. He used to go when he was young, and it was affordable. "I was a hippy." He had long hair and headed off on his motorcycle to Grateful Dead concerts. Francis is angry as he brings up the long years of redevelopment on the bridge, which have recently made life hell for the city's inhabitants. "Bayonne was an island," insists Francis against all the geographical evidence, "but the bridge turned it into a peninsula."

Perhaps the island he persists in describing to me is a metaphorical one. I am probably underestimating the poetic capabilities of this Trump voter. "It's a city of fucking

Democrats here. I love Trump! Yes, he's a multimillionaire, but he didn't take money away from anyone! I blame taxes! Taxes, taxes!" For ten minutes, Francis and I perform a play for which the script is already written. He knows it and he's enjoying himself; I know it and I'm bored. Fortunately, he's keeping an eye on his watch, so he can check his laundry. "I hate Clinton," he says to me out of the blue. "I hate her! We want her executed!" He's spluttering. "You're French, you know: I want her guillotined." And, all at once, I see pure hatred in the eyes of this ordinary man.

Finally, I manage to turn toward the young barman, a very attractive young man with beautiful tattoos. He tells me laconically that he was also born in Bayonne. "Welcome!" He smiles, as if to apologize for Francis, and offers us three Cokes.

So Bayonne, New Jersey, is not famous for anything, apart from the fifth-longest steel arch bridge in the world. And perhaps apart from its monument to the victims of September 11, recommended to us by the young barman. It is very difficult to locate, right at the end of the port area, well beyond Starting Point, and just before the golf course, which is open only in good weather. "Nobody here but me," says the caretaker of the golf course inside his little heated shed, which looks like a mini Swiss chalet. The clubhouse, on top of an artificial hill, looks like a Bavarian castle crossed with a Breton lighthouse. "Nobody here but me" could be the motto for the whole area, or the motto for us lost travelers.

The monument is a giant drip of nickel suspended inside a tall brick frame, the interior of which looks as if it has been torn away. It's something of a monstrosity, more than one hundred feet tall, resembling at best a tear, and at worst a saggy scrotum. This Tear Drop Memorial, also known as the Tear of Grief, has been the object of much derision. A plaque informs us that the monument, the work of the Georgian artist Zurab Tsereteli, dedicated

"To the Struggle Against World Terrorism," was a gift to the American people from Vladimir Putin, who traveled here for the unveiling on September 11, 2006, accompanied by Bill Clinton. Part of the tragicomic story behind this monument, which in the end I find moving, is connected to its initial homelessness. A *New York Times* article from September 16, 2005, recounts how Jersey City declined the offer when approached about the monument. It was supposed to be installed in Exchange Place, the district right opposite Ground Zero on the other side the river, but it was considered "too big" (not to mention too ugly). Several municipalities on the Jersey Shore passed the buck, until the city of Bayonne volunteered to take it. The mayor of Jersey City didn't hesitate to say, "Be my guest!"

"It's a weird city," says the guy at the bar of the Broadway Diner, where we're sheltering to get warm, a long way from Broadway in New York. "Half of this vast land was won on the water. Those Dutch and their polders. And it's a city you can never leave. It's a black hole. I've traveled all over the US, and there was someone from Bayonne everywhere I went. It's like the locals try to get away, but they inevitably come back. You see all those big cargo ships leaving, but you can never leave. I'm stuck here too. I'm a fireman, signed on for five years, but even then, I'm sure I won't be able to leave." A huge green neon light above our heads promises "The World's Best Pancakes." I ask the guy if he'd like to order anything, but he sticks with his coffee. "Call me Jimmy," he says, offering me his hand. I'm amazed that everyone here knows the other Bayonne. "It's because there's an exchange between the public high schools in the two cities. I went to the Catholic high school here. They're both good schools, we're lucky. But people here are weird, weird . . ." Jimmy repeats. "For example, a lot of them believe the water is contaminated with some sort of slow poison or hypnosis drug. And they're not necessarily wrong: with all the industrial chemicals, what exactly is coming out of the tap? And the rest of New Jersey makes fun of us. There's that awful joke: 'When you date some-one from Bayonne, leave him or her alone.' And when I was little, I used to watch a cartoon that was supposed to be funny—this was on national television—and one of the characters would say, 'Smells like Bayonne!' Tomorrow is the anniversary of the founding of the city—at the town hall. One hundred and fifty years on March 10. Are you coming?" But tomorrow is actually when I have to go back to France. Jimmy gives a shrug.

The two charming waitresses want to introduce us to a young girl they have gone to find at the back of the room. It turns out she is the German language assistant at the high school. There's a moment of confusion when we try to explain that German and French are not exactly the same. But the simple fact that we are European elicits enthusiasm. It's impossible to imagine this scene across the river in New York, or in any city accustomed to tourists. I chat with the waitresses. "You speak the most beautiful language in the world," one of them says to me over and over. She speaks five languages, but not French or German, even though she has a German passport; she's Turkish, born in Germany, emigrated here. Her female colleague is Puerto Rican; the cashier is a Chinese woman. Antoine, my daughter, and I eat a lot of pancakes with a lot of maple syrup, and order hot chocolates, which arrive crowned with whipped cream, in half-liter cups. "In France, you eat like birds!" laughs the waitress. Jimmy has to leave. We shake hands effusively. When we go to pay, we discover to our surprise that he has picked up the tab.

We decide to drop by the supermarket that has just opened, a Costco starting up in the same semi-deserted area where the ferry terminal will be built. It is quite sim-ply the biggest supermarket my daughter and I have ever seen. *America, the greatest country in the world.* Costco sells every conceivable product wholesale: groceries, clothes, toiletries, household appliances. For a start, the mayonnaise comes in three-liter jars, the cereal boxes sell by the dozen, and the shoppers all come in large sizes too. Neither the bodies nor the clothes resemble those in New York. The megamarket is clean, brand-new, the employees are smiling in their red T-shirts. The unemployment rate in Bayonne is 4 percent and rents are much lower than in New York, even if the real-estate pressure is increasing. My daughter is playing with a plush bear that is much bigger than she is; there are a dozen or so in a giant tub.

In the car, we listen to Elysian Fields. In 2000, in another time and in another world, before September 11, 2001, this rock band from Brooklyn wrote dreamy, cool songs for an ethereal voice. One song, called "Bayonne," seems oceans away from my own birthplace, better known for its bawdy festive songs.

The illuminated skyline of Manhattan rises slowly before us, along the winding roads we take to leave the port. There is nowhere else in the United States where I have felt so intensely the sensation of being "on the edge." Not exactly at the margins, because the people from Bayonne are neither poor nor disadvantaged, even if it seems they are inclined to be melancholic. But they are from the other side, the opposite shore, not even in the suburbs. They are at the end of the world, although the world is right in front of them. They make me think of the global destiny of all Earthlings: spinning around on a planet situated on the edge of the Milky Way—a luminous spiral that leaves us so far away on the outskirts that we see it as a ribbon—stuck on its shining periphery, far from the center.

THE
YELLOWSTONE
CHRONICLES

By
Joël Dicker

Translated by
Sam Taylor

The incident with the bear took place an hour earlier. I immediately went to inform the rangers, in accordance with the rules of Yellowstone National Park.

"As soon as I saw the bear coming toward me along the trail, I turned back in the direction of Mount Washburn. I passed a couple who were coming the other way and warned them about the situation. The three of us stayed together."

The ranger attentively notes down my story on an official report form.

"How did the bear behave?" he asks me.

"It continued advancing along the trail. It was catching up on us. I saw it panting and scratching the ground. So we left the path and went into the forest to let the bear pass. But it followed us. In the end it pretended to charge but stopped about two or three meters away from us."

"And what did you do?" the ranger asks.

"We managed to stay calm and we quickly took the lower path on the trail, but without making any sudden movements. The bear didn't move."

"Your reaction was perfect," the ranger says, putting the form down.

Next, he shows me the spot in question on a map to make sure that we are talking about the same area.

"Are you going to close the trail?" I ask.

"It's a possibility. It could be an isolated incident. But if something like that happens again, then we'll definitely close the trail. This is the bears' home."

I leave the visitor center in Canyon Village, in the middle of Yellowstone. Next door there is a gas station with a small general store where I go to buy some food. As I push open the door, I find myself face-to-face with the couple I met earlier. They are Texans, visiting from Houston. The man has just bought a can of anti-bear pepper spray, in case they meet another bear and things don't go quite so smoothly. The man vigorously shakes my hand and again expresses his gratitude.

"Thank you, Jerry," he says.

For the third time, taking care to articulate clearly, I correct his pronunciation: "My name is Joël."

"Okay. Well, thanks again, Jerry."

I smile. It doesn't matter. I wave goodbye and we go our separate ways.

I have been roaming Yellowstone for two weeks now. Two weeks spent sleeping in a tent and living side by side with wild animals in such apparent harmony that I stupidly let my guard down. Thankfully, that huge male black bear managed to give me a reminder free of charge: this is his home. There is no sharing here, something Yellowstone's visitors should never forget: nature merely tolerates their presence here. This place is completely wild.

For years, I had dreamed of visiting Yellowstone, eager to discover with my own eyes whether this legendary national park matched the image of it that I had formed in my head.

Yellowstone, located in the heart of the American West, straddles the states of Wyoming, Montana, and Idaho. It is far from the urban centers of New York and Los Angeles, where most foreign tourists flock. This is the old Wild West, the land of cowboys and miners, and I believe that nobody can really know the United States unless they have strayed beyond the narrow strips of coastline on either side to explore the depths of America's heartland.

My starting point is Denver, Colorado. From there, I drive for a day and a half to reach Yellowstone. I cross the state border into Wyoming, which proves a surprising and troubling place. The landscapes are incredible, but the towns through which I pass fill me with a mix of homesickness, boredom, and loneliness. The empty main roads lead into ghostlike industrial zones. With fewer than six hundred thousand inhabitants, Wyoming is the least populous state in America. And while it's true that it was the first state to grant (partial) voting rights to women, that was only to provide itself with enough votes to be officially admitted as a state.

These days, Wyoming is widely considered the most solidly Republican state in the country. The economy isn't strong, and many people here are in a precarious situation. To make things worse, the national coal mines were closed by Barack Obama as part of the campaign against climate change, but President Trump has promised to reopen them.

This is a long way from New York's melting pot: the population here is almost entirely white, and the people I meet give me strange looks. They ask about my accent and assume I must be German. "You're Swiss?" they say, surprised. "Where's that?" They ask me what I'm doing in Wyoming, and when I explain that I am on my way to Yellowstone, they don't understand why I am putting myself through such a long journey.

For the first time, I have the impression that I am far from civilization. Hours in a car or a plane from anything at all. Totally disconnected from the rest of the world. A feeling of absolute isolation. Whether I look east or west, there are thousands of kilometers of land, then thousands of kilometers of ocean between me and a different culture or a different country. Eager to arrive in Yellowstone, I speed along four-lane highways where I see nobody except for a police patrol car that flags me down. The cop gives me the same sort of a welcome that those intimidating sheriffs give to strangers in old Westerns. Finally I spend the night in a stale motel in a town with no name where, walking through a public park, I see some kids smoking cigarettes on a bench, facing a monument to soldiers from the town who died in the Korean War. It's hard not to wonder what that war could mean to them.

I drive through Wyoming on I-25 North, then take US-20 to Cody, the town founded by Buffalo Bill, at last taking Route 14 to Yellowstone's east entrance, one of five access points to the national park. Once I am past the rangers' checkpoint, the first few miles that I drive through look exactly like the landscapes that I left behind: the asphalt, covered in gravel from roadwork, is bordered by a forest. Nothing very impressive. I continue along the winding road, my view obstructed by mountainsides. At first I am disappointed: I do not feel as if I am anywhere special, but then I don't know what I was really expecting. Then suddenly, after a long curve, I find myself facing a vast plain of luxuriant grass, dotted with bison, stretching all the way to the horizon. It's so beautiful that it seems almost unreal. I park on the roadside and get out of my car to contemplate this vision of a lost paradise.

From that moment on, and during the three weeks that follow, I immerse myself in a world where flora and fauna flourish as almost nowhere else on the North American continent. I quickly understand that I am in another land altogether, and that the safety instructions given to me by the ranger when I entered the park are not only intended to preserve nature but, above all, to protect visitors: watch out for the animals, do not get too close to them, do not drop food, keep an eye on the weather. In the hour that follows, continuing along the park's only road, under the misleadingly placid gaze of the bison, I pass a wandering fox, a moose in a grove of trees, and a huge elk swimming in a river, all surrounded by a sublime landscape of immense trees and green prairies.

Entering Yellowstone National Park is a little bit like going back in time. In a world where nature is almost completely dominated by humans, Yellowstone—along with the neighboring national park, Grand Teton—is the last intact ecosystem in the north temperate zone, and the greatest expanse of virgin land in the United States, with the exception of Alaska. Man, here, is only passing through. This territory belongs to grizzly bears, black bears, wolves, pumas, coyotes, elk, bison, and deer. The sky is ruled by bald eagles and hundreds of other species of birds. As for the rivers and the lakes, they are the kingdom of otters and beavers.

Yellowstone is located on a plateau that rises to an average altitude of 8,500 feet, encircled by the Rocky Mountains, which reach as high as 13,000 feet. I knew the park was vast—it covers an area larger than Corsica—but I only really begin to comprehend it as I explore, discovering its endless landscapes. The borders of the park always seem distant, and each day offers me a breathtaking new backdrop: I pass from the Rocky Mountains to immense grass plains, from verdant valleys to arid canyons, from deep conifer forests to forests of petrified wood, from the icy water of mountain lakes and rivers to bubbling, sulfurous springs and geysers.

Yellowstone is the home of superlatives: here, you can find the greatest variety of species and the densest animal populations. The Yellowstone River, which gave its name to the park, is the longest river without a dam in the United States (excluding Alaska). Yellowstone Lake, in the middle of the park, is the largest mountain lake in North America. The petrified forest here is one of the biggest in the world. And to prove that it belongs neither to the East nor the West, Yellowstone is located on the watershed between the Pacific and the Atlantic. This means that, of the two great rivers that have their source in the park, one of them—the Snake River—ultimately flows into the Pacific Ocean, while the other—the Yellowstone River—travels all the way in the opposite direction before losing itself in the Atlantic Ocean.

What makes Yellowstone even more unique is its geological history. Beneath the park slumbers a supervolcano—one of the most powerful and potentially devastating volcanoes on the planet. Indeed, a large part of Yellowstone's land lies in a caldera: on top of a volcano that is not the usual conical shape, but flat. This caldera was formed by a massive eruption about six hundred thousand years ago; it was so powerful—three thousand times more powerful than Vesuvius when it destroyed Pompeii—that it would have covered half of the current United States with ash.

Yellowstone's supervolcano constitutes the biggest volcanic system in North America. Today it is not extinct, merely dormant, and nobody knows when the next eruption will take place. While it does not appear imminent, all the conditions exist for it to happen one day, with consequences that could well be global in scale.

The existence of this supervolcano was not discovered until the 1960s. Until then, nobody had realized that the more than ten thousand hot springs and three hundred geysers in the park were corollaries of a gigantic underground magma body. This discovery enabled scientists to understand that the sulfurous hot spring—with water temperatures of more than 158 degrees Fahrenheit—the fumaroles, the mud pools, and the gas emanations are all paravolcanic phenomena, sculpting the landscape in astonishing ways, making it look in some places like a furnace and in others like the surface of the moon.

The most impressive evidence of the supervolcano's existence is without doubt the spectacle offered by geysers, which occur when the phreatic zone comes into contact with the magma chamber, creating so much pressure that water spurts up into the air. Visitors from all over the world gather around these openings, waiting impatiently for the explosion. The busiest will stay in their cars and follow the road to the park's tourist hot spots: Norris Geyser Basin, which contains the hottest springs in the park; Mammoth Hot Springs and their improbable limestone statues; Grand Prismatic Spring, the largest known hot spring in the United States, with its fantastical blue and ocher colors; and, lastly, Old Faithful, the world's biggest geyser and the symbol of the park, which spurts water into the air every eighty-eight minutes on average, almost as reliable as clockwork.

But visitors who never leave the comfort of their cars deprive themselves of an incredible experience: that of discovering the park on foot, along the thousands of kilometers of hiking trails, which are the only real means of grasping Yellowstone's true power and sheer size.

It was during such a walk that I lived through one of the most memorable experiences of my life, in the wilderness of the Hayden Valley. On the western side of the park, this vast grassy plain, eleven square kilometers, is traversed by the Yellowstone River and located between Yellowstone Lake and Yellowstone Falls. It is undoubtedly the area of the park with the richest wildlife.

During my walk, as I come to the top of a hill, I see a ranger staring at the hill across from us. I stop and ask him what he is looking at so intensely.

"See that?" he asks, pointing to a dark shape that I hadn't spotted before, in the middle of the grass.

"Yeah. What is it?"

"A dead bison."

I grab my binoculars and immediately make out the head, which seems to stare back at me, and the motionless body.

"What did it die of?"

"No idea. But it's an incredible opportunity to see a carcass out in the open like that, because it means we can watch what the bears do to it, from a safe distance."

For now, there are no animals around the carcass. It's late afternoon and the ranger advises me to come back the next day, before dawn. I leave, and pitch my tent in a nearby campsite. As I settle in for the night, I discover to my horror that the batteries of my alarm clock have stopped working in the cold, and since I have no cell phone with me, I have no way of being sure to wake up in time. The only solution is to sleep on top of my sleeping bag. That way, I will be so cold that I will wake up regularly during the night, allowing me to check the time. This is what I do, breaking camp at 4:00 a.m. and heading for the hilltop where I saw the ranger.

On the way I meet another man, who has also been told about the carcass and wants to see what will happen to it. We walk side by side through the still-dark morning, talking loudly to alert any animals that can't see us, so we won't take them by surprise and risk being attacked. Suddenly, only a few meters ahead of us, a grizzly gallops past. The man next to me is armed with an anti-bear spray; he takes the safety off and keeps it ready in his hand. We feel nervous and extremely vulnerable in the total darkness.

Finally, at about 5:00 a.m., we arrive on the hilltop and make ourselves comfortable in the bushes. We will have to stay in the exact same position for the next four hours. I am lying on the hillside, wrapped up in warm clothing, nestled in leaves, my feet braced against roots. I follow the scene through the viewfinder of my camera.

As the sun rises, a cloud of crows is already twitching around the bison's carcass. Not long after, a grizzly appears at the edge of the nearby woods and, moving slowly and heavily, heads toward the heap of flesh. The bear starts biting chunks out of it. Then, with a precise swipe of its claw, it moves the dead body into a more convenient position. It eats for a long time, until a second grizzly appears. The newcomer, after weighing up its rival from a distance, decides to confront it. About thirty meters from us, the two bears fight tooth and claw. Finally, the second grizzly wins the battle and the first one slopes away, abandoning the dead bison, while the crows flap and caw all around.

The second bear spends a long time feeding on the bison before leaving the half-eaten carcass, presumably sated. We don't have to wait long before a third bear appears; clearly, it was waiting its turn. It comes out of the forest and hurtles greedily down the hillside to devour what is left of the meat.

When I look away from the grizzly for a second, I see a large gray wolf moving slowly out of the forest, followed by a second and then a third. Soon there are five wolves advancing stealthily down the hill. I can't tell whether the bear has noticed them or not, but apparently the wolves have no intention of attacking it. While four of them are content to observe the bear eating the carcass, the fifth— presumably the leader of the pack—approaches the bison and, taking advantage of a moment's inattention on the part of the grizzly, tears off a large piece of flesh, which it takes away to eat in the tall grass. When the bear is full, it leaves the remains of the bison to the wolves.

At 9:00 a.m., the sun starts to warm our observation post. It's a sunny day, and the animals will spend most of it in the shade of the forest. Soon the wolves disappear and all that is left behind is the bison's skeleton, picked clean by the crows, and its untouched head.

The first accounts of Yellowstone did not come from gold diggers—there was no gold rush in Wyoming—but from French-Canadian trappers, who were very active in the region at the end of the seventeenth century. In the early 1800s, they described the existence of this extraordinary place, full of valleys and waterfalls, hot sulfur springs and geysers, with a river running through it. In French, they named this place *Roche Jaune*, in reference to the yellow rocks of the Grand Canyon of the Yellowstone. This in turn was taken from the Hidatsa name: *Mi tsi a-da-zi*, "the river of yellow rock."

But the trappers' accounts were not taken seriously: newspapers at the time refused to publish them, certain that they must be pure lies and invention. It was not until November 1871 that the wider public discovered Yellowstone's existence, thanks to a story in the New York–based *Scribner's Monthly*. The magazine whipped up excitement among its readers with the publication of a survivor's account, entitled "Thirty-Seven Days of Peril," written by a certain Truman C. Everts, describing a month spent wandering through the Yellowstone territory.

Everts's adventure took place a year and a half before this. It is the summer of 1870 and he decides to take part in an expedition to map the region and evaluate its potential as a location for railway lines. Led by Henry Washburn, surveyor general of Montana, and Nathaniel Langford, a former tax inspector, the venture leaves Helena, the capital of Montana, on August 16. There are nine men in the party, including Everts. After six days of traveling, they reach Fort Ellis, where they are joined by a cavalry escort led by Lieutenant Doane. This troop has gone down in history as the Washburn-Langford-Doane Expedition, one of the first to explore the mysterious Yellowstone region in any real depth.

They travel up the Yellowstone River, methodically mapping every step of their journey. The expedition proceeds without any serious difficulties until the evening of September 9, when, setting up camp for the night, they realize that they are missing a man: Truman C. Everts.

Everts gets lost somewhere in the vicinity of Yellowstone Lake. He has no idea where the rest of the troop is, but at first he doesn't worry about it. He knows he will find them again easily enough. He is on horseback, with plenty of equipment and provisions. On the first night, he sets up camp alone, sure that he will meet up with the others the next day simply by following the river. But the next day, his horse suddenly escapes with all of his equipment and disappears, leaving Everts alone, without anything except the clothes on his back, some opera glasses, and two knives, both of which he manages to lose almost immediately.

Thus begins more than a month alone in the wilderness. Everts is completely lost, freezing cold, and starving. He gets chilblains on his feet after a snowstorm, has to sleep in a tree after being pursued by a puma, and scalds himself in a hot spring, suffering third-degree burns on his hip. And, just to compound his bad luck, when he manages to start a fire, he inadvertently rolls into it while sleeping and burns his hand. He somehow survives, despite eating almost nothing but a kind of thistle, which is afterward named in his honor. When a rescue expedition finally finds him on October 16, 1870—thirty-seven days after he was separated from the rest of his troop—he is at death's door: covered in burns and gangrene, hallucinating, and weighing only fifty pounds.

After a long, slow convalescence, Everts manages to recover from his ordeal. He refuses to pay the people who rescued him, arguing that he would have escaped the park himself. A year later, one of the Rocky Mountain peaks is named after him, and the publication of "Thirty-Seven Days of Peril" brings fame both to him and to Yellowstone.

By coincidence, in summer 1871, a few months before Everts's article appears, the first government-sponsored scientific expedition is sent by the US Congress to the Yellowstone region in order to find out more about this mysterious place. The expedition is led by Ferdinand Hayden, a geologist who had already explored the Rocky Mountains. With him are the photographer William Henry Jackson and the painter Thomas Moran, whose pictures of Yellowstone's landscapes will help convince senators of the unique character of the region and the necessity of protecting it by proclaiming it—on March 1, 1872—the first national park in the history of humanity, inventing the concept at the same time.

Thomas Moran's paintings, the authenticity of which is confirmed by Jackson's photographs, are then printed and seen by thousands of people, changing the public perception of Yellowstone: before this, the region was regarded as a hellish, dangerous furnace, but it gradually comes to be perceived as a place of enchantment and wonder. Almost a century and a half later, Barack Obama will choose a painting by Thomas Moran—representing a landscape of Grand Teton National Park, Yellowstone's neighbor—to hang on the wall of the Oval Office.

In its first year as a national park, Yellowstone welcomes a grand total of three hundred visitors. Ten years later, the arrival of the railroad in the region enables the annual figure to reach five thousand. During this same period, the Tukudeka tribes living in the Yellowstone territory are forcibly moved to a reservation near Wind River. In the early 1900s, work begins on the construction of the park's only road, which connects various points of interest. Today—155 years after its creation—Yellowstone National Park is visited by more than four million people every year, and the National Park Service rangers are responsible for supervising the tourists as they interact with nature.

As E. M. Cioran wrote: "At the zoo, all the animals behave appropriately except for the monkeys. One can sense that man is not far away." To judge by the moronic behavior of certain visitors, one might even wonder whether the greater danger is posed by wild animals or by human beings.

For a start, there are the road accidents: careless driving by tourists causes hundreds of collisions with animals every year. No fewer than ninety bison are killed annually on the park's road.

There is furthermore the generally imprudent behavior toward animals: visitors who, driven by curiosity, get too close to bison and end up gored; and badly managed encounters with bears, which are sometimes fatal. Then, of course, there are all the imbeciles who decide they want to take a dip in hot, acidic sulfur springs. In June 2016, a twenty-three-year-old Oregon man, visiting the park with his sister, ignored the many very clear No ENTRY signs and entered a dangerous zone. As his sister filmed him on her cell phone, the man thought it would be a good idea to put his finger into one of the pools so he could estimate its temperature: he fell in and died within seconds. The emergency services couldn't immediately recover his body due to weather conditions. When they returned the next day, the victim's corpse had been entirely dissolved by the water's acidity.

But when they are not busy trying to control people's thoughtless behavior, the National Park Service rangers devote their time and talents to scientific research and protecting nature by helping to monitor animal populations and maintain plant diversity.

Yellowstone has notably become a sanctuary for the bison of the North American continent, which were almost wiped out at the end of the nineteenth century after inhabiting the land for the previous million years. In 1902, there were fewer than fifty left in the park; today there are more than four thousand.

Wolves, too, were deliberately eradicated from the region in the 1920s because people believed they were harmful for the park's herds of bison. It was not until 1995 that wolves from Canada were finally reintroduced into the park. Observing the wolves' return to Yellowstone, scientists witnessed one of the clearest examples of a widespread "trophic cascade," the technical term for the ecological processes that have an impact on the entire food chain of a region and beyond. For seventy years, in the absence of predators, deer had proliferated, consuming a large part of the area's vegetation. The arrival of the wolves changed the behavior of the deer, which began avoiding certain parts of the park, notably the valleys, where they were easy prey. In those valleys, vegetation grew again, and in some areas the heights of the trees quintupled in six years. Places that had been stripped bare were suddenly covered with forests of poplars and willows, attracting large numbers of songbirds and migratory birds. The same thing happened with beavers, which started building dams on the rivers, enabling the formation of ponds and lakes, which in turn drew otters, ducks, fish, reptiles, and amphibians. Besides deer, the wolves also killed coyotes, leading to a rise in the populations of rabbits and mice, which in turn attracted more predators: falcons, foxes, weasels, and badgers. The carrion left behind by the wolves fed eagles and bears, which also increased in number, partly due to those carcasses but mostly because the reduction in the number of deer enabled the growth of trees producing berries, which bears love.

But the most fascinating observation made by the scientists at Yellowstone is that the wolves have changed the course of rivers. By enabling the growth of trees and vegetation along the banks, they have helped strengthen and stabilize them, limiting erosion and making the rivers straighter, narrower, and deeper. Thus, the wolves have not only transformed the ecosystem of Yellowstone National Park, they have also changed its physical geography.

Along with Alaska, Yellowstone is without doubt one of the most extraordinary places that I have visited in North America. If you are ever in the vicinity of Montana or Wyoming, don't miss the opportunity to discover the wonders of nature. Respect it, walk humbly among its forests and green valleys, admire the hot springs, the limestone sculptures, the astonishing geysers, the herds of bison, the wolves hunting in packs, and the grizzly bears patrolling the park. Enjoy the unique chance to visit one of the last remaining wildernesses on our planet, which your children and grandchildren may, sadly, never get to know.

HITCHHIKING
ALONG THE BORDER

By
Sylvain Prudhomme

Translated by
Jessica Moore

Juan is a taxi driver who lives on the Mexican side of the border, in Tijuana, across from San Diego, California. I get into his car around noon, after three or four hours of walking around downtown. I pay my way, of course, so it's not really hitchhiking yet—I'm cheating—but it's just so I can have a better chance of thumbing a ride later. I crossed into Mexico early this morning through the main border post, the one that lets out into the center of Tijuana, and I want to cross back into the States through the other one, at Garita de Otay, twelve kilometers east of the city. That's where the trucks cross, in the middle of an industrial zone. I'm hoping to find a big rig to take me eastward toward the Atlantic Ocean along Interstate 8 and then Interstate 10, the highways that cross California, Arizona, New Mexico, and Texas.

"Welcome to Tijuana / Tequila, sexo y marihuana." Songs by Los Tigres del Norte and The Buitres can be heard everywhere, and I discover that Manu Chao still has some smash hits too. Tijuana has changed in the past twenty years. Once a party zone for thrill-seeking Americans and other foreigners, the city has become more violent under the increasing influence of drug trafficking. The Sinaloa cartel controls this area, headed by the famous "El Chapo" Guzmán, whose extradition to the United States in January 2017 set off a bloody war of succession. The number of homicides rose drastically—758 between January and

April 2018, an increase of 67 percent compared to 2017. What strikes me most crossing the border is something unexpected—the omnipresence of medical establishments, flooded with thousands of Californians who come here every day to seek the medical attention they can't afford in the States. Dental offices, specialized clinics for cancer care, plastic surgery clinics, and pharmacies: medical tourism has begun to rival drug and sex tourism.

Juan and I drive dead east toward the maquiladoras, the factories that have sprung up all along the border to take advantage of the influx of cheap labor—immigrants from all over Central America end up here, ready to do any job in order to survive. I had imagined dusty old warehouses, but these are massive, modern, windowless crates, like the ones found in industrial areas all over the world. The maquiladoras produce everything: ready-to-wear fashion, electronic components, airplane parts. Evidence of the efflorescence of global capitalism, they are the property of big companies based in the United States, Canada, Japan, Korea, and sometimes Europe.

The road runs along the wall—the one that exists already, three to four meters high, whereas the one Trump wants to build would be at least ten meters tall. He's even said twelve or fifteen meters in some speeches. As our eyes slide along the length of the imposing barrier, Juan explains the symbolism of the innumerable planks of wood nailed to the wall: they are funerary crosses. Thousands of them, placed there by families, each for an illegal immigrant who died trying to cross the desert that begins a few dozen kilometers to the east. We pass the airport, driving under a narrow walkway that straddles the wall, a footbridge designed to facilitate tourist traffic—this way international travelers can come back to the American side without wasting time, explains Juan. The contrast couldn't be starker between the two worlds, the two sets of conditions, the two systems of freedom: crosses nailed to a wall for the people on one side, a raised walkway for the people on the other. "The most amazing thing," laughs Juan, "is that Trump wanted us to pay for it at first—he wanted *us* to pay for his wall." He points out some very tall warehouses on the American side. "Imagine—it would be as high as those buildings. All that for nothing. Smugglers are already digging tunnels. And for drugs, they have drones, submarines, and planes anyway. What difference would a wall make?"

Back on the American side, I walk two or three kilometers east toward the point where, in an Internet search, I spotted the first fragments of the wall: eight sample sections ten meters high, one after the other, like carpet panels hanging in a hardware store window. Two Border Patrol agents block the way. Beyond is the sierra, the desert of stones, the beginning of the great playing field where, every day, border guards and illegal immigrants play a deadly game of cat and mouse. One of the agents—José—stops me to ask what I want. I say something about the prototypes. He points them out, way out there on the far-off plains—I can just barely make them out. He lends me his binoculars so I can see them better. Is this hitching? Does the loan of binoculars from a border guard count as a ride offered? I decide it does. I take a photo of José and continue on my way.

At the entrance to Route 125, I get into Luis's 4x4. He comes to the States regularly for the avocado-import business he started three years ago, when he graduated from business school in Tijuana. Next, I climb into Mauricio's delivery van, filled with vacuum cleaners and pumps. Mauricio is also Mexican but has permanent-resident status in the US; though he doesn't believe in the wall, he does think something has to be done. "We can't very well take on the healthcare costs for everyone who enters the country illegally," he says, alluding to Obamacare. He seems glad that Trump has quashed the program.

Then there's the aptly named "Great," who screeches to the side of the road, picks me up, and takes off again like a shot. He's African American, originally from Chicago, talks really fast, gets annoyed when now and then I ask him to repeat himself. There won't be a photo of him, he tells me early on: "You can write whatever you want but no picture, okay?" He tells me I'm crazy to be hitchhiking: "People are evil. People will kill you. And they'll do it with a smile, that's the worst part: they'll smile at you and at the same time, *bam*, they'll kill you." Right. And besides that, I ask him, everything's cool? He stops once, twice, three times, for the time it takes to pick up an envelope, to bring it into a snack bar or a store, to come back again . . . After three such stops, I put it together that he's delivering: "Weed. Weed, obviously, man!" He holds out a little plastic box for me to smell. Recreational cannabis is legal in California. "We fought for that. We went to see all the old guys, everyone we knew, we went door to door to explain to them that they had to vote for legalization." Great is thirty-nine. He fought in Afghanistan and Iraq. He was one of the Marines who held the Baghdad airport. The phone rings—he answers, looks at me, and apologizes. "Man, I'm gonna have to go back to Spring Valley, I've got a delivery to do there. But after that I'm going your way, I swear. You wanna stay with me or get out here?" I picture myself gathering dust on the shoulder of the road. I stay. "Cool," he says. We do a U-turn and head back toward San Diego. Once the delivery is done, we pass a park. Great asks if I want to go smoke one with the big dudes chilling there, dealers even more burly than he is. "You want to taste some true San Diego? You want to experience the real West Coast?" He laughs when I check the time. "That's your loss, man." I get out at a rest stop, the Rest Area of Boulder Oaks—which is actually just some miserable porta-potties under the on-ramp—a cul-de-sac where no one stops. It's 5:00 p.m. I still have two hundred kilometers to go before Yuma. I'm in the middle of nowhere.

I wait a good hour among the desert hills and stones, solitary birds of prey circling overhead. I refuse a ride from a fat man with a pasty complexion and greasy hair who says I can ride with him so long as I strip down too. "You can come with me, but look, I drive naked," he tells me, lifting his belly with both hands to show me he's not kidding. Then I meet Hector, a computer equipment technician for primary schools in San Diego. He commutes every day from Calexico, where he lives, on the border facing Mexicali—twin cities whose mirrored names are a symbol in themselves, a symbol of the incessant exchanges between the two countries.

From El Centro, I catch a ride with Shelvy, fifty-eight, whose dust-covered car looks like it's been through a storm of plaster and rubble. There's a jumble of tools, plastic rims, and hub caps in the back. "Sorry about the mess, but I'm a mechanic, so . . ." He's one of five employees in an El Centro garage specializing in repair of the buggies, quads, and Jet Skis that abound on and around the Colorado River. I enter Arizona with Shelvy. We pass through magical landscapes—deserts of stones, then dunes, then stones again. I discover the Imperial Sand Dunes Recreation Area, the site where a number of scenes from Star Wars were shot, and where, once the season opens, up to two hundred thousand quad drivers gather. Shelvy knows the names of the trees and plants, and he tells me about the countless flowers that bloom in these dry lands at the first spring rains. At times the road runs alongside the wall, clearly visible here, hugging the curves of the hills a few hundred meters away. The Camino del Diablo—the Devil's Path—is very near here: one of the most well-used routes for illegal immigrants. One of the deadliest too, since water is so scarce and the heat brutal. Border Patrol cars are everywhere—they track would-be immigrants day and night now, sometimes driving up to one hundred kilometers into the territory. Mexicans? Shelvy has nothing against them. But he doesn't hide the fact that in El Centro, there are two worlds: "There are lots of them, the city is split in two. There's us and them"—and I understand that this "us" means white Americans, who speak English, who often feel they're being overrun, and who voted for Trump.

The next day I ride for a good two hours with Mélanie and Martin, Mexican residents who work in real estate. They admire Trump's chutzpah—"He has balls!"—but find most of his actions absurd. They rail against the financial waste of the wall and the recent move to send soldiers as backup along the border, "thousands of guys who know nothing about the area and won't do any good." They also talk about the gun madness in America: "Sure, people settle scores in Mexico, too, but do crazy men open fire in a high school for no reason?"

At Gila Bend I meet José, forty-nine, a mason, who says possibly the most profound thing I'll hear about Trump: "The giant of racism was sleeping peacefully—all Trump did was wake it up." He calls him "El Trump." José builds houses for pro-Trump white Americans and sometimes even for Border Patrol agents, who, like everyone else, he laughs, employ illegal immigrants. "I swear, the same illegals they spend all day trying to catch. Even his stupid wall—if he makes it happen, who's gonna build it? Us, of course. Mexican immigrants. And there will be some illegals among us, that's for sure." He himself came into the United States illegally in 1986, "when it was easy." José, like 2.7 million other immigrants, benefited from the vast legalization bill signed by President Reagan that same year. Even today, economists recommend the Immigration and Control Act because of the economic benefits these undocumented immigrants bring to the nation. José talks about the difficulty of crossing without getting caught, of the five or six terrible days that illegal immigrants face before arriving in a safe space, especially those who don't have much money and can only pay the minimum—around $6,000, the sum that *los coyotes* demand nowadays to smuggle people, called *los pollos*, "chickens," which says a lot about their vulnerability. "The more money you pay, the less they make you walk. People who can afford it can arrange to be driven part of the way. They get meals and barns to sleep in. For the others, it's six days of avoiding the patrols, a bad fall, snakes, and the heat."

We're in the middle of Tohono O'odham territory, not far from Yaqui territory, two Native American peoples for whom the wall would be another humiliation: "They've been living on horseback between Mexico and Arizona forever. It would be like cutting them in two." But José is hopeful for the Dreamers—the eight hundred thousand undocumented immigrants who grew up in the United States and who were allowed to stay in the country under Obama's presidency. Now Trump wants to deport them. "It's crazy, they came here with their parents, they grew up here—they don't have any other country besides the United States. Plus, almost all of them are highly qualified, hard workers. Trump won't win this one." José is a philosopher. He loves talking about life, and celebrating the fact that, in spite of everything, it's pretty sweet—*suave* in Spanish. "Ay Silvano! We were lucky to be born in this life. What do you say—life is beautiful, no?"

A sad motorist with tattooed arms in Tucson doesn't see things this way. He parks his truck in front of my NOGALES sign and looks me up and down with disgust. "What the hell do you want to go to Mexico for? There's nothing there. It's ugly, it's dangerous—there's nothing but thieves and drug addicts. You want to get killed, is that it? I hope you have a gun at least." I imagine this is what is meant by white trash: a white person who's racist and proud of it.

*   *   *

Next are two mythical border cities: El Paso and Ciudad
Juárez. Juárez is where the Mexican Revolution started in
1911 with Madero and Pancho Villa; and Juárez is also
where people have been traveling from Mexico into the
United States forever by crossing the Rio Grande, which
the Mexicans call the Río Bravo. It's here, across the border, in El Paso hotels overlooking the Mexican side of the
river, that spies, outlaws, businessmen, and journalists from
everywhere have always kept watch on comings and goings,
sniffing out trouble. More recently, Ciudad Juárez, population 1.3 million, also became known as the "murder capital
of the world," with a record of three thousand homicides
just in 2010—including an exceptionally high number of
murdered women, most of them female workers who came
here alone to work in the maquiladoras. This is the terrible state of things: lack of guilty parties convicted, omertà
imposed by the cartels, atrocious abuse inflicted on the victims. Several documentaries, TV series, films, and books—
beginning with the novel *2666* by Roberto Bolaño—have
attempted to tell the story of *feminicidio*, "femicide."

I reach Juárez by way of the fenced-in bridge on the
border. From above, the contrast is spectacular: on the
El Paso side, huge buildings catch the eye and draw an
insolent, dominant skyline against the backdrop of hills;
on the Juárez side, tens of thousands of tin roofs and ram-
shackle electrical connections sprawl, and no monument
stands out, aside from a mural dedicated to Juan Gabriel,
the famous singer of the city. On one side, glass and marble facades, verticality, newness, shininess, the promise of
opulence, the Wells Fargo sign legible from dozens of kilometers away; on the other, the labyrinth of overpopulated
colonias, alleyways as far as the eye can see, the cloud of
pollution, every last inch of ground covered with buildings, at the foot of rocky hills adorned with the words
"The Bible is truth. Read it." Below, the mythic river, the
Rio Grande—which springs forth from the Rockies and

rushes three thousand kilometers downstream, marking the border all the way to the Atlantic—is nothing but a thin trickle of brownish water between two banks reinforced with concrete like a sewer drain. Cameras, barbed wire, walls, fences, Border Patrol cars lying in wait every fifty meters: the cities touch, infinitely close and intensely separate at once. FUCK TRUMP, says a tag beside a drawing of the White House with a wall all around it.

In Juárez, it's a sunny Saturday in April. The pedestrian avenue that leads to the cathedral and to the market, entirely car-free, is incredibly lively. I hear Hector before I see him. Mainly, I see the hundreds of spectators amassed in a circle around this thirteen-year-old kid, cheering. He's in the center, microphone in hand, wearing a suit, his face proud, beaming at the ovation. He sings his heart out, *corridos* and other Mexican love songs, in grand lyrical style, amplified by two powerful speakers. It's beautiful. It transports me as much as the drivers I have been riding with—I count this as a trip. A little farther on there are duos, sometimes a full orchestra—perhaps a dozen ensembles altogether from the end of the street up to the cathedral—*norteños*, electric rock, mariachi guitars. I was a little nervous when I got here. But now, against all odds, I have the feeling of coming back to life after the dreadful boredom of the streets of El Paso. Families buy balloons, sweethearts eat churros and shrimp cocktails with tomato and avocado, a group of high schoolers take selfies in front of a mime. Same buzz of activity at the market. Fruits and vegetables, clothes made in China, *chicharrones*, cell phones, school supplies, toys, religious knickknacks, T-shirts dedicated to the glory of the "Santísima Muerte," the Reaper worshipped by narcos and mafiosos. I see bordellos, too, with large colorful signs to attract customers. Everywhere, things are stirring, people coming and going, buying and selling, drinking and eating, chatting, living life. "*Hay movimiento*," as the Mexicans say. In the paper, I learn that five murders were committed the day before. Even so: things are moving, and it feels good.

Farther east, I hit the south of Texas. This is cowboy country, and the beginning of Route 90. I get a ride with Simon first, who talks about the Bible; the apostolic community of which he's a member; his father, a pastor in Juárez; and the righteous ones who paid with their lives for having told the truth—Jesus, Lincoln, Kennedy, Martin Luther King Jr., and Pancho Villa. "Trump says he doesn't want any more illegal aliens, but who was here before the arrival of the Americans? Who were the first inhabitants? There was no one but brown-skinned people here. It's the whites who came illegally." He doesn't want his photo taken—this would be the sin of pride—unless I take it "without his permission," a kind of contortionist pact he offers, which I accept and which results in an almost-brutal picture, in which he's protecting himself from the lens.

After Simon, there's Macario and Nelly, also Mexican residents—like almost everyone who has helped me from the start. They're headed for Midland—the oil stronghold of the Bush family—where Macario works behind the wheel of a giant cement mixer beside a drill that digs new wells each day—some more than seven thousand meters deep. Next, I meet Armando, in charge of maintenance of the glass roof over a tomato plantation where all the employees are Mexican—two thirds of them without resident status. "They get up at five each morning, do the round trip from Mexico by bus, one hundred kilometers from here. If not for them, who would do the work?" He smiles. "There's only one white person on the plantation: the boss."

Farther on, in Marfa, an elegant little town where minimalist artist Donald Judd set up an art foundation, I get into the sublime Lincoln of the artist DonJon Vonavich, wearing a cowboy hat and leather boots. I will drive nearly four hundred kilometers with him. Of course he hates Trump, makes fun of and trash talks him. "Obviously he's racist. But not racist like an illiterate person from the South. You could say he's even more classist than racist. He hates poor people more than anything. If a black person succeeds, if he makes a good living, he has his place in Trump's America." DonJon has seen the world of finance up close—he made his fortune in the 1990s and lost everything in the crash of 2000. At the moment, he's appalled by the ever-increasing gulf between rich and poor.

We reach Sanderson, a stone's throw from the spot where the hero of *No Country for Old Men*, the Cormac McCarthy novel made into a film by the Coen brothers, picks up the suitcase full of money abandoned after the narcos kill each other. From a bin of dollar-a-piece clothing, DonJon unearths a gorgeous cowboy hat and gives it to me. The landscapes are majestic, the sky immense. After five hours, I get out in Del Rio, walk past the Regal Motel, and think about stopping here; but I end up continuing on, hitching a ride to Eagle Pass, one hundred kilometers farther down the road. That night as I rewatch parts of the Coen brothers' movie, I realize with a jolt that the motel the motel where I almost stopped is the very same one where Josh Brolin hides the suitcase of money, and where Javier Bardem comes to find it, bottle of gas and shotgun in hand. I would have thought the motel would capitalize on the movie to attract tourists, but the shoot-out that follows must not have seemed like the best publicity. The Regal Motel remains a basic motel, forty dollars a night.

The next part of the trip is a gentle slope down toward the Atlantic coast. Among the drivers who pick me up, there's Emiliano, my first truck driver, returning from a delivery of solar panels near Dallas. Then Laura, as I'm coming back from a visit to the Mexican side, in Piedras Negras, where her husband used to live—he passed away seven months ago. Next is David, a carpenter, mason, electrician, and also a singer. "Or rather, singer-songwriter, since singer by itself wouldn't be quite true: I don't sing particularly well—my wife even accuses me of singing off-key. Whereas songwriter is true. Even if I'm all alone in my room, I write songs!" Victor, my second truck driver, drives a red race car he's repainted himself. He likes his job, makes $1,400 a week. "I get paid to travel around, what do you think of that?" I meet him as he's on his way to pick up his truck in Laredo. From there, he will take deliveries to Michigan, Mexican-made carbon-fiber staircases—"bought by Trump, I imagine, to stop the Mexicans from using them to scale his wall!" he jokes. A Border Patrol car passes us, white and green as they all are, and he points to it and says: "You know what we call them, among us? Green beans."

Laredo is as depressing as Juárez was delightful. This whole eastern zone has become the most dangerous area of the border. Two all-powerful cartels fight for control of the *plazas*: the Gulf cartel and Los Zetas. The news headlines are grim: confrontations between narcos and soldiers are an almost daily occurrence. Forty percent of all US-Mexico trade passes through Laredo—the largest commercial port in all of Latin America. The largest drug port, too, inevitably. I walk through the streets, on both sides of the border, until evening falls, without ever finding the *movimiento* of Ciudad Juárez. I've barely arrived on the Mexican side when a white car with tinted windows pulls up. A man gets out, impeccably dressed, with slicked back hair and an immaculate white T-shirt. He asks if I need any drugs—"whatever you want, I've got everything"—tells me he can deliver it to the American side the next day. His car follows me for a moment, weaving behind me through the traffic. Then finally disappears.

I head off again with Belinda and Rodolfo, a stay-at-home mom and a house painter, then with Roberto and

Hector, who let me ride in the back of their pickup for the next three hundred kilometers. At one point when I'm having a hard time getting a ride, a guy passing cheers me on: "The whole border zone stinks, man. You're in shit. No one will pick you up. Because no one trusts anyone here." When I arrive in Brownsville, I have only forty kilometers left until the sea. The last legs of the trip are with Maria, a graphic design teacher who traveled alone in Europe when she was twenty and from that trip retains the conviction that we shouldn't fear anything in life: "We should be careful, yes, but we should always remain open, always have trust." Then with Dror, an Israeli who lives in a religious community in South Padre Island with three generations of cousins and relatives, sixty people in three houses. Ironically, I only learn what he does for a living as I'm getting out of his car: he's an ICE agent. In the air deportation service. "Just today, we took sixty Mexicans back." He's the one I should be asking about Trump's wall, what he thinks about it, about the Dreamers, the eleven million undocumented immigrants on American territory, who, if legalized, would help the GDP to increase by 20 percent. The truth about the drug-trafficking industry is that billions of dollars are laundered by American banks in Dallas and Houston, profiting several high-profile politicians and businessmen in both countries. Ed Vulliamy reported on this in the 2010 movie *Amexica*.

Finally, South Padre Island. I head for the beach: it's massive and deserted in the fading light. I watch the waves. The Atlantic. Two lovers are entwined on a plastic chair. They are the only other people as far as the eye can see. The next day I catch a plane to Matamoros, the capital of the Zetas cartel on the Mexican side. Getting into Alfredo's taxi, I can feel that he's tense. Just as I'm about to take his picture, I ask if it's a bad idea. "That depends," he says, smiling, "on whether you want them to kidnap us both. The downtown is small here. Everyone notices when a stranger arrives." He shows me the cathedral, tells me the narcos set off a bomb in front of it one day when the street was packed. "Just to show everyone that they're here. To say it's in everyone's interest to pay the *cuota*, the tax, without protest." We're driving slowly through the narrow streets of downtown. "The mafia controls everything here. All of Mexico is ruled by the mafia. Even the politicians are mafiosos. They're just a different kind: accredited mafiosos, with license plates!" We pass several cars stamped SEGURIDAD PRIVADA, probably the most booming business in the city, and the one with the shortest life expectancy. Police cars too, that look more like tanks than regular vehicles: a heavily armed man in a bulletproof vest surveys the scene through the open roof. You'd think you were in Iraq.

I leave with this final image of the border: one of tension, fear, and real prevailing violence. On my way back to France, a stopover in the wild energy of Los Angeles only heightens, in contrast, the lasting impression of the cities I've just traveled through as poor places, hard places. Places where there's little room for pleasure. Where life is toilsome, harsh, and precarious. Where many people are busy just surviving, others trafficking, and still others spying on the traffickers, dodging those who spy. And something else occurs to me: the rides I was offered, the hospitality, the warmth, were almost entirely from Mexican residents. How many white Americans have picked me up in this whole trip? Two, maybe three at most, out of about thirty. The ones who did were tremendously welcoming, but rare. And yet—white Americans do exist and are even numerous, statistically. Particularly if we reduce the target population to drivers, as in my case. How many passed right by me, often alone at the wheel, careful to keep their distance? When we get down to it, there's a consistency here:

they are the ones who want the wall to be built. In the latest news, at the end of May 2019, Trump confirmed that it would be built, and quickly: "We don't have a choice." He even chose the sample he liked best, said José, the border guard who lent me the binoculars in San Diego. "The one farthest to the right."

FOUR LETTERS FROM
AMERICA

By
Laura Kasischke

"One Love Letter"

Dear Woman Ahead of Me in Line at the Grocery Store in October,

I love you. We've never met. You were paging through *People* magazine while we waited for yet another woman to get her boxes of frozen waffles and cans of tomato juice out of her cart and onto the moving belt, so that another woman could pick them up and pass them over the supernatural eye that would read our products' abbreviated names and prices from a code that we ourselves would never be able to read because it was not a message for human beings—and you were not, yourself, a machine.

You found the page you'd been searching for, and stopped, and then I was looking at you looking at photographs of other people in *People* magazine.

In profile, you looked tired, and the lipstick you'd applied, perhaps carefully in a bathroom mirror earlier that day, had faded.

There were expressionless people in the magazine, many of whom had other people bending over them, who were looking around, desperately, as if trying to find something they'd lost, while also appearing to have forgotten what it was.

And there were people who were wounded, it seemed, being helped by friends, or maybe perfect strangers—everyone hurrying and completely silent as they screamed.

Then, I watched you stare for a longer time at a photograph of a girl wearing white cowboy boots: both of the girl's knees were red and wet (had she fallen on concrete and scraped them as she ran, or had she recently been kneeling in someone's blood?), and who had, too, a lovely pale-purple manicure, which I could see because the elegant fingers of the girl's right hand were covering her mouth as she appeared to wail or shriek, either wildly or without sound.

You put the magazine back into the rack from which you'd taken it, slipped it in with the others, neatly into the place where such magazines are kept—very purposefully kept at the eye level of a woman of average height, one who has found herself frozen in time, waiting for her turn in a checkout line, where such a woman might grow curious, bored, pick it up, and maybe decide to spend $5.99 more than she'd expected to spend, on a magazine she hadn't expected ever to want to read that day.

But you never even glanced at Khloe Kardashian & Tristan Thompson: BABY ON THE WAY.

The woman behind the cash register had grown impatient:

"Ma'am?"

Maybe you'd forgotten where you were by then, or why you were there, or maybe you'd lost track of the custom of being in a hurry, so that you'd failed to notice that the woman ahead of you was pushing her own silver cart out of the aisle already by then, toward the doors, which were opening automatically for her with a yawn, while, for you, everyone was waiting.

"Oh my God," you said, "I'm so sorry," to the cashier, and then you looked behind you, to apologize to me, and to the woman who stood behind me, too, who was kind enough to wait until you'd turned around before she rolled her eyes about you, at me.

We were all about the same age, or so it seemed to me, or at least we were that day. There were no younger women, no older women, either, and the only man was elderly, fumbling around with a twenty-dollar bill, trying to force it into a slot so he could purchase a lottery ticket, become a millionaire.

Except for him, we were probably all mothers, but to teenagers, or to grown children. No emergencies there. We'd all stopped on our way home from work because, as usual, we were out of everything we needed. And, as always, the civilization in which we lived together was bright and loud and colorfully brief. But, of course, if you looked too closely at it you could also see how everything was a little dirty. There were fingerprints on every shiny surface. There was dirt ground into the cracks between the tiles on the floor. The music wasn't being played from the ceiling to entertain us, or even to distract us. It was simply a habit, which had to do with commerce. No one remembered why it was being played, or for whom, since no one could have heard the song itself unless we'd all stopped at once, someone had said *shhhh*, and we'd each held our breath while tilting our ears toward the ceiling—and this would never happen.

Still, all of us were standing at the same time on a flat surface, together. It was like a board that was being balanced on something round and hard and small, like a child's rubber ball. If one of us moved just a little too far in one direction or the other, that board was going to tip over, and then we'd all be tumbling off it into whatever dark emptiness or flashing television commercial was waiting for us at the edges of this particular time and place.

We were, of course, in terrible danger, since none of us seemed aware of this, so we moved mostly without any consideration for the consequences, and certainly with no awareness of how those consequences would be shared by anyone else.

Except for you, my love:

I tried not to stare, but I could see it . . .

You were the one upon whom the rest of us depended, while you remained unaware of it, simply buying a bag of apples, a carton of yogurt, and one tomato that looked to me to be pink, rock-hard, mealy—another tomato that had been taken off the vine too early, shipped too far in a refrigerated trailer—and which would never ripen now, would always be inedible.

Oh, you had a few of the other things we all come to the grocery store to get, like paper towels and cooking oil, tinfoil and ketchup, because we're always running out of them. And it would all add up to more than you'd expected, more than you could afford. But, as your items were being swiped one at a time across that all-knowing and all-seeing eye, you turned around, and said, to me, "Excuse me," as you reached past me and took the magazine off the shelf again, placed it on the belt, watched it slide into the cashier's hand, and then saw the flash of its purchase registered up there with all of the rest.

Now, it's under a bed or in a drawer in the house or apartment in which you live. Likely, you won't ever even open it again. But, that girl, a total stranger, with her pretty face turned into a mask of anguish—you took her with you while the rest of us sighed impatiently.

You even apologized.

I loved you, and I will always love you, and I know we will meet one day, very soon, again.

Yours truly,
America

"A Thank You Note"

Thank you for coming, and for staying. Thank you for praying to your gods, however deaf they were, however strange.

Thank you for the civil discourse, even when it was too violent, or too vague. Thank you for trying to explain all of this to your children. Thank you for not explaining. For hate, thanks. And for love, when you were crawling on your knees, or when you refused to crawl. Also thank you for the fireworks and parades. Thank you for picket lines, riots, angry radio tirades. Thank you for the gift of tongues, and tithes, and for your obscenities, and for intolerance, and for staying all night when we begged you to stay for the rest of your lives to play charades. Thank you for the celebrities who laughed with their martinis in their swimming pools before they died, and for setting your cars on fire when you won or lost the football game. Thank you for the hate (did we thank you for this already?) and for the intolerance (stop us if you've heard this one before), and for electrocuting an elephant, and then for filming it so we could watch it, in horror, a century later, and marvel at ourselves, while staring aghast at ourselves as you—and how, from this, we learned cruelty, and learned kindness. Also thanks a lot for all the bullets, for the handcuffs, for the flags you waved, and for burning the flags. And the big cars. The big breasts. The green lawns in the safe neighborhoods, and the stray dogs in the bad neighborhoods where children lived, grew old, and died. Thank you for Ma Barker and her boys, killed in a shoot-out with the FBI. Thank you for making that seem romantic at the time. Thank you, later, for allowing us time to realize . . .

Like the fan in the window.

Like the sky: an unsettling blue.

Like the woman who ate only chicken and lived to be a hundred. Like cigarettes. Bubblegum. Like the scars from the shrapnel, and from the whips. Like the open wounds from the chains around the necks. Thank you for the glamor, for the poverty—that they might look at each other on television, and marvel, and learn: something.

(What is it?)

Oh, remember? It's something like this: that if you look into the dazzling screen too long the dazzling screen looks back at you.

Oh, and thank you for resisting the temptation before giving into it. Thank you for not answering the telephone before you answered it. Thank you for voting—whether or not you did. Thank you for your service, and for your wars, and for your lip-service, and for your drones. And thank you in advance for your forgiveness—whether or not you deserve it, now, if you ever did.

Finally, thank you for coming, and staying, and for taking us down, brick by brick, now and then.

We look forward to seeing you again someday.

In the meantime, thank you for reading this.

Yours truly,
U.S.A.

"A History Lesson"

On January 25, 1989, in an American town that prefers not to be named, the corpse of seventy-three-year-old Robert Hann was found in a trash can on his own front porch.

Look: who can be blamed for this? The old man must have crawled into it because he'd thrown something away that he wanted to get back, and now we'll never know what it was because he got stuck.

We'll never know, either, how many people mistook his situation for something it wasn't; however, we do know that the mailman saw him waving, and that the mailman waved back, because the old man had always been friendly, and the mailman was friendly, too.

We also know that a Girl Scout selling cookies ran home to tell her mother that she'd seen something strange—a man in a trash can on a front porch, a man who asked her politely if she could give him a hand. But we also know how children exaggerate. And that her mother was busy, had dinner to make, while the Girl Scout had homework to do, or was late for ballet.

The records and the recollections tell us that it was unseasonably warm for January that year, so Hann was able to survive for several nights. Still it was January, and the man was dressed in pajamas.

We know that many others saw him waving, and that they waved back, too, and shouted hello as they biked, or strolled, or drove their cars by his front porch slowly before he died.

He seemed to be attending to business, they said, but was still not too busy to be friendly.

But, as noted, he was in pajamas. So, being polite, no one wanted to embarrass him by lingering, by asking questions. Everyone has a right to privacy. It's a free country.

And we know that most (but not all) wished—after hearing that he'd been dying for several days, on his own front porch, in his own trash can—that they'd been paying a little more attention.

"Message in a Bottle, from America, Tossed into the Ocean"

HI! HOW ARE YOU? I'M DOING GREAT. SOMEONE HAS SEWN THESE BIRDS TOGETHER BY THE TIPS OF THEIR WINGS. HOWEVER. THAT'S ALL I CAN SAY. THAT, AND FROM WHERE I'M STANDING TODAY I CAN SEE THEM RISING ALL TOGETHER INTO THE SKY—WHETHER BY FORCE OR BY CHOICE. SUMMER SOON. LOOKING FORWARD TO IT! THE ROSES WILL START TO BLOOM AND FROM A DISTANCE THEY'LL LOOK A LOT LIKE CHILDREN'S BLOODY LITTLE HANDPRINTS ON A

WALL. SUMMER, LIKE IT ALWAYS IS. WELL, HAVE A GREAT DAY! I DON'T KNOW YOU AND YOU DON'T KNOW ME AND BY THE TIME YOU GET THIS I DON'T KNOW WHERE YOU'LL BE OR WHERE I AM, IF ANYBODY EVER FINDS THIS AND EVEN READS IT. BUT I'M DOING FINE UNTIL THEN! JUST SAYING HI BECAUSE THAT'S ALL THERE IS TO SAY!

CHOCOLATE-COLORED
WASHINGTON

By
Abdourahman Waberi

Translated by
David and Nicole Ball

Foggy Bottom

Sometimes, in the middle of the semester, my American students have a rather strange feeling, halfway between dread and wonder. They express it with a loud *wow*, repeated every time I teach the course in modern French literature to my undergrads. Charles Baudelaire is the cause of this feeling of awe, a subtle feeling, one difficult to convey in another language, and to pass along from one culture to another. This surge of adrenalin is not insignificant: it comes from the distant past. Facing the changes Baron Haussmann imprinted on the Parisian landscape, Baudelaire captured the emotional reaction to the profound upheavals underway. Just two lines from the *Fleurs du mal* say it all: *La forme d'une ville / Change plus vite, hélas ! que le cœur d'un mortel*: "The shape of a city / Changes more quickly, alas! than the heart of a mortal." And now my students, mortals barely out of adolescence, swept along by the limitless wind of optimism, are suddenly struck by the precariousness and fragility that underlie the shape of any city and, in the end, any form of life.

I am a child of the city. The countryside is foreign to me. Meadows and lakes, canyons and the bush, I know nothing of all that. Born over half a century ago in a Djibouti slum, I spent my adolescence exploring the other part of my city: the white, colonial city, so close and yet so foreign. I mean, of course, the French city with its well-behaved blond children, its inaccessible beaches, its military camps, its white arcades, and its Legionnaire bars. As I became an adult, most of the white city's values became part of me, and through them I discovered different, more distant worlds. I became a nomad as much out of taste as necessity. Nowadays, Caen, Berlin, Boston, Rome, Paris, and Washington, DC, are a thousand times more familiar to me than the savannah and hinterland of the Horn of Africa once plowed by my nomadic ancestors.

Nothing had predestined me to settle in Washington, DC. I make my little burrow here and I've come to love this city, open to the four winds of the world. It is said that DC was designed by a Frenchman, Pierre Charles L'Enfant, who came here at the end of the eighteenth century with Marquis de Lafayette. He was right to give pride of place to wide thoroughfares and large natural spaces: today they are the trademark of the capital. Anyone who watches even the opening credits of the famous TV series *House of Cards* can get a fair idea of the topography of Washington. A city of power, the Rome of modern times, the capital appears as a world made of illusions and dreams, a separate, parallel universe that is also somehow familiar. Kevin Spacey is perfect as Frank Underwood, a member of Congress who will stop at nothing to get to the White House. The charm of his wife, Claire Underwood, magnificently played by Robin Wright, is not the least considerable asset of this diabolical husband whose cynicism and opportunism know no bounds. Lasting about a minute and twenty seconds, the long credit sequence beginning each episode became an immediately recognizable hit. It may have changed ever so slightly with the series' subsequent seasons, but it still leaves an imprint on the retina and cortex, just as it did on the very first day. Whoever has heard the soundtrack to this credit sequence, concocted by the composer Jeff Beal, cannot possibly forget the solemn trumpet and drumrolls over the ever-changing sky or the smooth, glittering surfaces of the empty city.

Washington is not just a city; it is also a metropolitan center for three regions—the District of Columbia, Maryland, and Virginia—a visual patchwork. According to the US Census Bureau, this urban area houses 4.5 million inhabitants, which makes it the eighth largest in the country, behind New York (18 million) and Philadelphia (5.4 million) but ahead of Boston (4.1 million) and Baltimore (2.7 million). Washington is also a world city: wealthy and straitlaced on the one hand, wretchedly poor and rebellious on the other. You can find everyone here. Rich, even very rich families—particularly in nearby Bethesda. And poor and very poor households, in Prince George County, for example. In the imagination of Washingtonians, that county, commonly called PG, holds the same place that the diverse urban district north of Paris called "93" has in the imagination of Parisians.

I lived and taught for five semesters in southern California, at Claremont, a small college halfway between Los Angeles and San Bernardino. The singer, composer, and multi-instrumentalist Ben Harper was born in Pomona, where Claremont College is located. From there, I landed in Washington at the end of the summer of 2012. I immediately turned my back on southern California, its eternal summers and unparalleled aridity. I found my oasis here; I don't want to go anywhere else anymore. I took up my post at George Washington University (GWU, for those in the know), in the heart of the historical neighborhood of Foggy Bottom, characterized by its very dense network of political, economic, and cultural institutions, private foundations, ministries, and monuments.

My university takes up the larger part of Foggy Bottom, and its strategic position is highly enviable. Of course, GWU's field of excellence is international relations. Here, immersion is not a plan to be carried out or an image to be converted to actuality. It's a palpable reality for all our students. Large international organizations such as the World

Bank and the International Monetary Fund are nestled inside the perimeter of our main campus. The slim silhouette of Madame Christine Lagarde, the chair of the IMF since 2011, is a familiar sight. It instantly suggests Parisian elegance. But that isn't all. My university has an asset like no other. It is three blocks away from 1600 Pennsylvania Avenue. The inner sanctum. The White House.

Built on marshy ground, caressed by the Potomac, Washington is all curves and gentle hills. But don't be fooled by its appearance. From my first week, I felt the force of attraction emanating from our powerful neighbor. My student Gladys felt that attraction, too. I can't forget her face, always beaming in any weather. She was then taking my "Black France" course, while simultaneously interning at the White House. Round, jovial, and enterprising, Gladys says she felt her energy triple when she met her mentor: Michelle Obama. She told me of the kindness and legendary charisma of the First Lady. Gladys would give anything to keep on fighting at her side against the countless ills of junk food.

Another student from that semester, Leah, volunteered in a Senate campaign in Massachusetts. A Democrat named Elizabeth Warren, who was not yet well known, had just challenged the incumbent senator, who was backed by the former governor Mitt Romney, the future unsuccessful candidate in the 2012 presidential election. Leah had joined the team of the former special adviser to President Barack Obama because, she told me, Elizabeth Warren had conceived and founded the new Consumer Protection Agency and made it an important actor on the national stage.

These two students joined the fight of two women who were both challenging powerful lobbies and trying to improve the wellbeing and health of their fellow citizens. The more Michelle Obama and Elizabeth Warren were attacked and disparaged by conservatives and Wall Street, the more Gladys and Leah defended them. Naturally, in that fall of 2012, I had other students who went knocking on doors for the reelection of the president. Still others went once or twice a week to the nearby Salvation Army center. Wearing white gloves and a paper chef's hat, they served hot meals to those people who'd been knocked around by life and came there to get a bowl of soup and a roof over their heads for an hour or a night. Winter and summer, the homeless are always there—often black, former jailbirds dragging their big bundles of belongings, red-eyed addicts, the mentally ill talking to themselves, veterans haunted by far-off wars, prostitutes of all kinds, teenagers with big bellies, grandmothers with tattooed lips—all part of that suffering humanity that zigzags around the capital of the most powerful nation in the world.

My students have remained my guides, as you can see. I learn so many things when I talk to them. I make use of everything they share with me. I let myself be carried away by their enthusiasm. Below their youthful appearance, they're often burning with an authentic thirst for justice. I listen to my young informants with infinite pleasure. With my senses awakened, I collect—often without realizing it— the little details that comprise the fabric of most ordinary American lives.

My students come from all over the country, from the fifty states of the Union, as well as the District of Columbia and Puerto Rico. They also come from China, Europe, Latin America, Africa, and the Persian Gulf. My students are at GWU to feel the pulse of the nation. To take their share of the immense political and media power concentrated in this little piece of land called DC. But that doesn't make them dupes. They are very aware of the dangers that the weight of big money and the entertainment industry pose for the life of a democracy. They know they're privileged, or have been up to now. "So far so good," as they say. What will tomorrow be like? That anxiety is there, lurking in their hearts. It's visible, too. It shows in every conversation. It comes up in jokes, even in bursts of laughter. Unemployment, student debt, and a drop in their socioeconomic status—but the words are never said explicitly.

It's been five or six years since I've seen my students of 2012. Gladys and Leah. But also Mike, Katelyn, Calvin, Ben, Elliott, Juliana, and the others. Some stayed in Washington to pursue their professional careers. Others went back to their home states, the foreigners to their own countries. They contact me if they need to. A request for a letter of recommendation here, a New Year's card there. Sometimes, an e-mail comes to me from Paris. Joy and warmth. And there's the merry-go-round of memories. I put my head between my hands, close my eyes, and take some deep breaths. Two or three long ones. I open my eyes, keep my inner calm, and time rises back to the surface.

How far away that first semester seems now! So many things have happened. Obama ended his second and last term in the middle of nowhere. Hillary Clinton lost the election, even if she got more votes than her opponent. And *he* barged in. He's still here, can you imagine? He thinks he's presidential—yes, him! *Oh my God*, he occupies the marble palace. One would so like to forget him, to erase him once and for all. Because he's a madman. Or an idiot. Or both. William Faulkner couldn't have imagined such a disaster.

That's how people talk about Donald Trump, at least in Washington. Here, nobody voted for the Manhattan billionaire. The District is a Democratic fortress. No wonder, it's the seat of federal power and the administration. Washington is the traditional bogeyman of Republicans and libertarians, who vow to put anyone dressed in the suit of a civil servant on a strict diet. For every demagogue, Washington is a synonym of Gomorrah. As a candidate, Trump portrayed it as a stinking swamp, to be drained immediately. He would set about it from his first day in office, he said.

In these first days of February 2019, the gulf between the president and the population of the District is deep and not likely to be filled anytime soon. We had to endure the *shutdown*. The shut*what?* To the French, the word is as incomprehensible as the thing itself. It suggests the paralysis of all the organs of the state. The closing of all agencies, the freezing of civil servants' salaries. The shutdown is a kind of aberrant breakdown, hard to grasp anywhere else in the world. Of course, it can be avoided with a little common sense or political will. But it's a nightmare, especially in Washington. The threat of a shutdown hangs over Capitol Hill. It is rarely put into action, but the mechanism becomes a weapon of mass destruction when the two chambers of Congress can't manage to find a political way out. This time, Americans went through the longest shutdown in their history. It began on December 22, 2018, after President Donald Trump, motivated purely by revenge, rejected the budget bill presented by Congress. The reason: the billions of dollars required to build a wall between the United States and Mexico had not been granted by the Democrats, who now controlled the House. The shutdown ended on January 25, 2019. But it could start again at any time.

Aside from the threat that still hangs over the heads of civil servants, and aside from its exceptional length, the shutdown took place, from start to finish, in a toxic atmosphere. The figures are mind-boggling: eight hundred thousand federal workers kept working without salary for thirty-five days, as did millions of contract workers. The total financial loss to the economy exceeded $11 billion, according to a congressional assessment. The long-term effects remain unknown. And no agency was spared. Imagine a country with most of its national museums and parks, customs offices, and public records offices closed. Who can picture Paris without the Louvre or the Palais de Tokyo, without the supersleuths at 36 Quai des Orfèvres, Matignon (the prime minister's office) emptied of its civil servants,

the big ears of our intelligence agency on the Boulevard
Mortier gone deaf, the Metro closed, no buses running,
no postal workers or garbage collectors?

All that happened in Washington and in the four
corners of this vast country.

Do you need an example? Okay, let's talk about
national security, a theme dear to President Trump's heart.
Tim O'Connor, the head of the FBI Special Agents Association, sounded the alarm as early as mid-January. The
thirteen thousand agents of the Bureau managed to work
somehow, but their mission became harder and more dangerous every day, he warned. What's more, he called the
American people to witness, playing on their patriotic feelings. And yet, the shutdown went on for two more weeks.
Those who opposed it shouted and demonstrated. The
president's supporters didn't budge an inch. Days followed
weeks. And little by little, we became used to a situation
previously unheard of, as if it were straight out of a bad
propaganda film. Every weekday at noon, Washington's
civil servants lined up and had to show their ID in order to
get a meal on a tray offered by a charitable organization.
The lines grew longer by the day. At first they felt bewil-
dered, then powerless and ashamed. The private sector
became worried, too, as the health and defense sectors
depend on federal subsidies. In this subregion, the cabinets
in charge of these two sectors employ a large number of
people. Whole cities depend on them, like Pentagon City,
next to the famous Arlington National Cemetery.

Logan Circle

At GWU, a private university, certain programs were put
on hold because federal funding stopped. The summer
will be catastrophic, the administrators whispered as they
waited for spring. The homeless population of Logan Circle
was also waiting for spring. The first time I crossed Logan

Circle, I thought of Sepha Stephanos, the main character of *The Beautiful Things That Heaven Bears,* Dinaw Mengestu's first novel, published in 2007. Sepha is an Ethiopian immigrant who settles in Washington, and more precisely in the half working-class, half affluent neighborhood of Logan Circle. Between two daydreams, he runs a small grocery store. He spends the little free time he has with his friends, Africans like himself: Joseph, a Congolese man who's a waiter in a restaurant; and Kenneth, a Kenyan man who became an engineer. The novel unfolds in little touches—sensitive, melancholy, and philosophical. True, this little community lives modestly, but it moves freely. It can dream of better days to come.

"There is something unsettling about spring in DC, a cautionary tale of overindulgence and inflated expectations that seems embedded in the grass and in the trees. I thought I had long since learned to keep those expectations in check, but it happens anyway, doesn't it? We forget who we are and where we came from, and in doing so, believe we are entitled to much more than we deserve."

Without any grand effects, Dinaw Mengestu captures the essence of a life or of an era. In those days, few people in the immigrant community knew the name of Donald Trump. And things were just fine that way, Sepha, Kenneth, and Joseph would add in chorus.

I should say that Dinaw Mengestu, who now lives in New York, was once my compass in Washington. He helped me understand the city better. Born in Addis Ababa in 1978 and taken to the United States two years later, the future winner of a MacArthur Foundation "Genius" award grew up in Peoria, Illinois—that is to say, in the middle of nowhere. You think I'm just being facile. Judge for yourself: this good-sized Midwestern town was a favorite target of humorists in the last century. Peoria is so typical, there's a legend about it. Not exactly a legend, but rather a saying. That town acts as a lab test. If some product appeals to the people of Peoria, the rule goes, it will sell everywhere else. Whatever the product—a shampoo, a woman in politics, a stage play—the prognostic remains the same. The question "Will it play in Peoria?" is the only thing that matters. The answer promises to make pollsters and marketing nerds rich.

Dinaw Mengestu knows Washington inside out. He's a graduate of Georgetown, a university founded by the Jesuits. With its campus in the heart of the eponymous historic village, this wealthy institution is a reflection of the distinguished society of yesterday and today. An impressive number of American political figures—from Bill Clinton to Madeleine Albright—as well as foreign ones—from the former Spanish prime minister José María Aznar to the former Colombian president Álvaro Uribe—studied or taught there. As for the native of Addis Ababa, he first studied there and then returned as a teacher. He held a position at Georgetown University for three years before he flew off to other skies. During his tenure, he invited me twice to meet the students who were taking his course in creative writing. I remember one discussion in particular. Dinaw told us how he captured the voice of the narrator in his first novel: "One night, as I was walking around the streets of Washington, I saw that Ethiopian immigrant behind the counter of his tiny grocery, and his voice never left me." There was long pause, the time for the maestro to retrieve the thread of his story: "Of course, I come from a family of immigrants. As long as I pay attention to the women and men around me, I can succeed in capturing the meaning of their lives. These people are looking for a roof over their family's head, a school for their children . . . Which is, I think, a deeply human, universal aspiration."

If the story my friend Dinaw Mengestu tells strikes a chord in his students, it's because it reflects millions of other stories told by millions of immigrants who left their home on foot, by boat, by train, or by plane. Aside from the Native Americans and the sons and daughters of black slaves, all the other groups of Americans are descendants of immigrants. Some fled famine, like the Irish, and others, pogroms, like the Jews from Russia. Only the points of departure have changed. If he were still alive, Karl Marx would doubtless have written brilliant pages on the importance of this inexhaustible human capital, which powers this gigantic machine spanning more than a continent—the United States of America.

It is said that the largest Ethiopian community outside Ethiopia itself lives in Washington: 250,000 people strong. This isn't a reliable figure, just an estimate. Yet on the ground, such an estimate doesn't seem exaggerated. Hail a cab at Union Station and you have a good chance of coming across a driver with an aquiline nose and Abyssinian features.

U Street

"As African Americans, we're both admired and envied in France," Erika announces. She's one of the students who have just returned from Paris. Born and bred in Silver Springs, a suburb of DC, she defines herself as a pure native of America. Erika loves the comedian Dave Chappelle, a Washingtonian like herself; and soul food, the culinary tradition that black mothers have been able to preserve and transmit from generation to generation, a thousand miles from Uncle Ben, the innocuous character invented as a brand by the food-processing industry to sell a long-grain, quick-cooking rice.

Erika kept a diary during her study-abroad semester in Paris. It's February, Black History Month, and she wants to share her impressions: "It took me some time to understand the way people acted with me and the marks of attention they paid me. Believe it or not, prof, we enjoy a visibility in the world that other black people of the diaspora don't have—Cubans or Brazilians, for instance. African

Americans represent everything that's cool, they're the true creators of hip-hop, the icons of pop culture. They make buzz all the time. Our celebrities, like Nicki Minaj or Pharrell Williams, are celebrities over there, too. Our favorite TV shows are their favorites, too. African Americans make their voices heard against injustices and inequalities. Everybody there knows how Eric Garner and Trayvon Martin died. Martin Luther King Jr.'s "I Have a Dream" speech is known by the French, the Italians, and other Europeans. The slogan Black Lives Matter rings out all over the world and the Civil Rights movement is known to all the students, like it is here. African American history has left a clear mark on everybody's history. My experience in France made me prouder, believe me, prof!" Erika's optimism is sincere.

Back in DC, she's glad to find her native land again. Slightly apprehensive, too. Despite eight years of Barack Obama's presidency, nothing has changed, or almost nothing. Her community has the same problems. And tourists are struck by the wretched poverty on Capitol Hill, its alleys, dark from afternoon on, its many liquor stores and its derelict silhouettes. It would be as if, once you'd strolled past the Élysée Palace—the president's residence in Paris—you found yourself all of a sudden in the most underprivileged parts of Paris or Marseilles. The White House and the black ghetto on the same esplanade. Glitz and magnificence on one side, hopelessness and hunger on the other. And between these two worlds, no checkpoints, no barbed wire. Just broad, windy boulevards. A troubling proximity.

This is a dichotomy Erika knows very well. She moves through it with grace and dignity. She keeps her anger for other struggles. Washington hardly deserves its old nickname of "Chocolate City" anymore. Latinos hold the northern part of the city now, around Columbia Heights. Part of the Adams Morgan neighborhood and the corridor of U Street, where the ghosts of Dizzy Gillespie and Marvin Gaye still hang out, is called "Little Ethiopia." Gaye was born in what used to be a mecca for the arts. But that's not all. White yuppies bought up whole blocks of houses that were once the pride and glory of the black elite of Howard, the leading predominantly black university in the country. This phenomenon of gentrification is not isolated: you can see it all over the country, from Harlem to the Crenshaw neighborhood, where much of the Los Angeles black bourgeoisie used to live. All in all, the black population of Washington has melted, dropping from 72 percent in 1970 to 51 percent in 2010.

Across the centuries and the oceans, the melancholy lines of Baudelaire evoked at the beginning of our narrative recall another line by the late lamented Gil Scott-Heron, the subject of my 2015 book *The Divine Song* (*La Divine Chanson*), a novel in the form of an homage. In 1977, he raised a moving stele in Detroit, not only the former capital of the automobile industry and heart of black music, but also a city with a black majority. "We Almost Lost Detroit," sang Gil Scott-Heron. This cry tears at the heartstrings of Erika's parents—and the heartstrings of every Washingtonian of their generation.

TRANS-
AMERICA

By
Alex Marzano-Lesnevich

I n my house, the bills all come to Alexandria—but it is Alex who pays them, Alex who makes the coffee and pours the wine, Alex who sleeps and showers and fucks and sits at the desk to write.

A year ago, I changed the name I went by in the world. *Alexandria*, the name that had always before been mine—a name that I still like, even think pretty—had never quite felt like me, more like a costume, the way the words *girl* and *woman* and *female* have felt, for as long as I can remember, like being called the wrong name. The change had been a long time coming. At eight years old, I had understood clearly that I wasn't a girl. The problem was that the only other option I had back then was being a boy, and I needed only to look at my twin brother to know that *boy* wasn't right, either. For decades I carried this conflict with me always, my life like a set of clothes that didn't quite fit.

I was in my thirties before I understood that there was, actually, language for how I felt, for who I am: *Nonbinary. Genderqueer.* I just hadn't heard the language before. The words felt frightfully new to me—could people really just declare who they were and claim language for it?—but when I looked to history, I found that there have always been people who identify this way. They have gone by different names in different cultures and at different times, but there have always been people for whom the strict gender binary of male versus female never really fit.

Still, claiming this language as my own felt impossible for a few years. In part, the impossibility felt tied to what I'd lived as a child. As a little girl (yes, I still think of my childhood self that way) I'd been sexually abused by my grandfather, and then barred from speaking about it by my parents. Now I wanted to change my name to reflect my identity, but to erase the name *Alexandria* before ever putting my childhood into words seemed like it would deny the child I once was a voice, permanently and forever.

Then I wrote *The Fact of a Body*, the name *Alexandria* on the cover of the book. I wrote about my family, about the abuse that had happened, and about a legal case that had long fascinated me. Publishing that book changed my life in many ways. It made me a public person. It gave me a career as a writer. But the biggest and most unexpected change by far was this: When I first held the published book in my hands, I realized I had made a place for the past to live. I didn't have to testify to the experience of the little girl Alexandria anymore—the book could.

I recall that moment starkly. Holding the book, I sobbed with relief. It wasn't just that after years of researching and writing, my dream of being an author had come to fruition. It was that without betraying Alexandria, I could get on with the business of being me. *Alex* is what I had insisted on being called as a young child. To seize it as my name again felt like a reclaiming. In the year that followed, I came out as genderqueer, part of the trans community.

Doing so felt, without exaggeration, like oxygen after a long time deprived. Alex stood up straighter, spoke more confidently, carried themselves differently. Alex seemed to shed the thin film of unease that had clothed and cloaked me for as long as I could remember. I had always assumed that the unease was the residue of abuse, and I'm sure some of it was, but not all. So much of it was gender, being forced into a category that didn't suit me. How quickly the unease melted when I no longer felt marked as *female* just by my name. I cut my hair off, I bought new clothing from the men's side of the store, I asked friends and acquaintances and even strangers to use the gender-neutral pronouns *they/them* for me. I became, almost instantly, happier than I had ever before been in my life. My life suddenly my own.

But of course it wasn't quite that simple. It couldn't be. Our lives are not only our own. We are individuals, yes, but we are also part of the societies in which we live. Though the person referred to by the names *Alexandria* and *Alex* was and is one and the same—though I am the same person I have always been—society seemed suddenly to want to shove me to the margins. Three times, men pushed into me on the sidewalk, screaming threats of rape into my face, threats of what they'd use their body to "fix" about mine. Cars slowed on the street, men leaning out windows to shout at me. People made rude remarks or asked inappropriate questions about my body at the gym, at the university where I teach, at the supermarket, as I stood in line for vacation ice cream with my girlfriend. When I published an op-ed in the *New York Times* about what interacting with airport security is like for trans passengers like myself, strangers telephoned my office to tell me that trans people didn't exist—that I was wrong about who I was, that I was confused, that *I* didn't exist. Overnight my body became a contested space: endlessly commented on, endlessly up for debate.

This has all been as exhausting—and as infuriating—as you might expect. I am me; what is so difficult to grasp about that? But I am aware, too, that part of my shock is simply how new the experience of others trying to marginalize me is. I am white. I grew up in an upper-middle-class suburb and was raised by two affluent and educated parents. I went to graduate school at Harvard, and then proceeded to teach there. I am now a professor at one of the most prestigious colleges in the United States. True, I'm gay and have long been publicly out, but society had changed enough by the time I was an adult that my queerness was never as marginalizing an identity as I once feared it might be. I simply have not experienced the discrimination that black and brown members of American society have. On the contrary: I've been raised to expect that my voice should be heard, to expect that others will want to hear it, and to expect access to, and power in, the mainstream.

So let me use that voice now to tell you a story. And that story is simply this: people like me have always been here.

Fifty years have now passed since the famed Stonewall riots of June 1969, the riots that are the reason LGBTQ people all over the world celebrate Pride Month in June. On June 28, 1969, transgender and queer patrons of the Stonewall Inn, a small, grungy bar in New York City's Greenwich Village, fought back against police harassment and raids. No one knows who was the first to resist, to throw a punch or toss a beer bottle, but in the weeks of clashes with the police that followed, trans women of color, like Sylvia Rivera and Marsha P. Johnson, earned the nickname *trancestors*—a portmanteau of *trans* and *ancestors*—and their fight ushered in a new era of visibility. Visibility, rather than existence. Again: we have always been here.

That the Stonewall riots took place in June is why rainbow flags now break out all over the world that month, from the streets of Alaska to the streets of Paris, from South Africa to Bangkok. I was in Dublin for Pride this year, and nearly every shop window displayed its wares in rainbow colors. Every bank hung banners. Pride has become so commercialized—and so mainstream—it's easy to forget that the first Pride demonstration was an anti-police riot, or how much change is still needed, how much discrimination and hate still exist. Instead Stonewall is thought of as a magical beginning, the beginning of a new world in which rainbow flags now fly and people like me can be ourselves. A world in which what was once on the margin has become mainstream.

But to think of Stonewall that way—to think of history that way—is to tell the lie of the margins. The lie of the margins is the lie of newness, a lie that says a marginalized group is brand new and has never before been encountered by the mainstream. The word *trans* is modern, yes, but trans people are not only modern. The historian Peter Boag has documented extensive histories of gender nonconforming individuals on the Old West frontier, the mythical heart of America. Other documented cases date back to colonial settlers.

The lie of the margins is that the margins are anti-tradition, and a threat to that tradition. But whose tradition? As historian Thomas Laqueur has argued, the very idea of there being only two binary genders, and of those genders as fixed and immutable by biology, is relatively new in historical terms. Sex and gender were understood very differently in the early 1700s and before, and in that sense, a truly traditional understanding is not as rigid as the more modern fixity. (Nor is the strict gender binary that so dominates the West the only way of understanding gender worldwide. Again: whose tradition?)

The lie of the margins erases power. It pretends that those on the margins just are there, have not been pushed there. But history reminds us that history is a story told by the victors—and thus the marginalization of the marginalized is erased.

We confuse, it seems to me, the margins with the marginalized. In Trump, the United States elected a man who is in love with saying others are on the margins, that he is in the mainstream. When Trump attacks young congresswomen of color, telling them to "go back" to the countries they came from, what he is saying is *you are on the margins, you are not central, the real America is a thing other than you*. But the congresswomen are, of course, American citizens, elected in America, by Americans, to represent America. All but one was born in America. And all of their biographies are more characteristically American than Trump's is.

Just moments after Trump was sworn into office on January 20, 2017, language acknowledging the existence and rights of LGBTQ Americans vanished from the White House's website—just vanished, as though the Americans themselves had been erased. Under what the National Center for Transgender Equality rightly calls "the discrimination administration," the federal government has withdrawn laws protecting transgender people's access to healthcare and housing, banned transgender people from serving in the armed forces, and removed protections for our safety. The crackdown happening in America—the deep and vile hate—against not just trans people but all minority groups is part of a profound lie of America, a lie that says there was once an America that didn't have trans people or people of color, a lie that defines the margins as those who are marginalized by the mainstream rather than those who cling to an antiquated and imaginary idea, a lie that would push America back to a time that never truly existed.

As the writer and thinker bell hooks once wrote, maybe then the way to think about the margins is instead to think of them as a space of vision and possibility. To be told that you are on the margins is to be able to see the lie and to refuse it. To imagine another way.

Next week, I will go renew my driver's license for the first time since moving to my new state of Maine. When I do so, my identity—who I am—will suddenly become legitimate in the eyes of my state. Maine, like eleven other states in the US, has documentation that recognizes nonbinary genders. I will hand the clerk a form that indicates

I identify as nonbinary, and they will mark my gender as X. For the first time in my life I will be named as who I am.

My United States identification—my passport—still will not, however, reflect my gender correctly. I doubt it ever will in Trump's America.

But to correctly see history is to know that history does not end here.

A HAT IN
MANHATTAN

By
François Busnel

Translated by
Kate Deimling

"Y ou're holding the most famous hat in the history of American literature." Gay Talese grabs me by the shoulders and stares straight at me, his eyes shining with excitement. I have in my hands a cream-colored fedora with black trim from Jay Lord Hatters, the premier New York hatmaker.

Five minutes earlier, the owner of the aforementioned hat calmly walked down the few steps leading to East Sixty-First Street, closed the wrought-iron gate behind him, waved to the driver who had been patiently waiting for several minutes, and disappeared into a big black SUV that instantly dissolved into the flow of traffic. Did memories stirred up by our interview fluster him, or was he simply tired on this hot, humid afternoon? Whatever the reason, Tom Wolfe forgot his indispensable headgear, and his friend Gay Talese is all in a tizzy. What if he has a dinner invitation? Or a party to go to? An unexpected visit? Or what if a photographer just happens to surprise him getting out of the car with his head bare? Tom Wolfe—a man who doesn't overlook a single detail, whether in his books or his appearance, always the picture of a Southern gentleman in his trim white suit—without his legendary hat? The thought is outrageous. "Un-*think*-able!" our host harrumphs.

I suggest a solution: "Maybe I could return it to him. My hotel is right near his place. Since it's getting late, I

could leave it with the doorman so as not to disturb him."
Gay Talese frowns. His bushy eyebrows are straight as hor-
izontal dashes, and his hair is thick and silvery. In a dark
suit fitting his svelte figure like a glove, he looks like a Cal-
abrian godfather. "OK," he finally agrees, as if granting a
favor. And this is how I end up schlepping Tom Wolfe's hat
through the streets of the Upper East Side.

A blast of hot air greets me on East Sixty-First. The
sun skims the skyscrapers, and Park Avenue is empty except
for some cabs cruising slowly along. A whole slew of famous
people that no one's ever heard of live in this neighborhood
that's dead after 7:00 p.m. The old New York, spared by the
hustle and bustle of the rest of Manhattan. Walking north
up the avenue, I remember how Tom Wolfe described it in
the early eighties:

> . . . kheew!—the sun blasts them in the eyes and there it
> is, wild, childish, bald, overpowering Park Avenue in the
> Fifties, huge cliffs of plate glass and steel frames, like a
> mountain of telephone booths. Hundreds of, jaysus, mil-
> lions of dollars' worth of shimmering junk, with so many
> sheets of plate glass the buildings all reflect each other in
> marine greens and blues, like a 25-cent postcard . . . the
> sheer incredible yah!—we've-got-it money and power it
> represents. The Rome of the twentieth century.

Here it is, then, the true symbol of New York: not the Statue
of Liberty or the Empire State Building, not Wall Street or
Times Square, but a two-way divided street far from the
tourist mob. Wolfe and Talese, who have been New Yorkers
for over seventy years, have become masters in the art of
uncovering Gotham's countless secrets, and describe their
city like no one else can. New York, "where millions of the
wretched are washed up," Wolfe wrote. "The heart of the
whirlwind of money and power," Talese added. "La crème
de la crème," they both aver, smiling.

It was Tom Wolfe who suggested we meet at Gay Talese's home. The idea was to talk about the two of them, Trump, the American taboos they have been unearthing since they were old enough to hold a pen, and what literature can do in an era like ours. Plus, of course, the famous "New Journalism," which they invented and still represent today—especially since we're all wondering how to write about what's happening now, and how to separate truth from rumor in an age of what the president calls "alternative facts" and "post-truth." Their influence is perhaps not quite as important as it once was, but their legend still precedes them. Today's most prominent American journalists —even if they may be skeptical of the pair's recent literary output—recognize that these two transformed the profession like no one else. William Finnegan, who has written for the *New Yorker* for thirty years and won the Pulitzer Prize for Biography in 2016 with his excellent book *Barbarian Days*, sums up the status of Wolfe and Talese in a few simple words: "Their impact comes from their boldness. They both stretched the limits of fiction and reporting while holding up the truth as an insurmountable horizon. They are still absolute reference points and powerful landmarks."

What do these two princes of nonfiction have to tell us? I expected to see two wise men on this summer's day, but instead I encountered a couple of straight shooters with their tongues firmly planted in their cheeks. Gay serves Tom a big glass of sparkling water, then mixes two martinis. They won't get us smashed, but they're strong enough for us to sink back into the sofa cushions and let the target practice begin. "Do you really want to talk about Trump and this country?" asks Talese, with a hint of sarcasm in his voice. "I *like* Trump." Wolfe leans over and taps my arm. "Let's wait a little while, it's a sensitive issue." OK. We'll wait. For a little while. How long have the two of them known each other? Their eyes look skyward. They try a date— "1963?"—then look for another—"Wasn't it 1959?"—and dig through their memories for ten minutes looking for hidden clues. I watch them watching each other. They stare at each other as if checking to see what damage time has done, and I wonder if they are partners or rivals. A bit of both, most likely.

Wolfe, at age eighty-six, and Talese, at eighty-five, make one hell of a duo.* They're both dandies with exquisitely delicate manners. Gay Talese is tall, with sharp features, a skeptical glower, and an irreverent attitude. His suit was tailor-made by his cousin Cristiani on Rue de la Paix in Paris. This Italian tailor's son is dignified without being starchy. As graceful as a faun, he is warm and funny. A bit of a ham, too. As soon as he can, he hijacks the interview and deluges his friend with questions about his life. Wolfe nods his head and replies politely, in a frail voice. But something has changed. He has difficulty walking. His back is stooped. His hair is thinner. I look at his hands gripping the armrest. They're covered with spots, twisted by arthritis. Wolfe has aged a great deal since we last met, only a year ago, when his photo appeared in all the newspapers and magazines celebrating his books along with his personal style. "Sometimes I tell people who see me like this that I just turned 104. They're very touched. All of a sudden, they have more to say to me. . . ." With this remark, his steel blue eyes start to sparkle again and a smile appears on his thin lips, turning into a sharp little laugh. Tom Wolfe never complains and has a rare talent for self-deprecation, pulling his pants leg up slightly to show Talese his white-and-black socks, which look like piano keys. Today, he's wearing a cream-colored flannel suit, one of thirty-two that are custom-made for him by Vincent Nicolosi, the tailor at 501 Madison Avenue. His shirt, black with fine white stripes and a starched collar, is from Alex Kabbaz in Amagansett,

---

* This article was published in 2018, based on a 2017 conversation between Busnel, Talese, and Wolfe. Tom Wolfe passed away on May 14, 2018.

the white enamel cufflinks are from Tender Buttons, two blocks away, and his two-tone shoes are available only at George Cleverley, in London. "Style makes the man," Wolfe and Talese both maintain, and their suits remain perfectly crisp after four hours of conversation. "Today, sloppiness starts with attire. So it's no surprise that it spreads to the brain," Gay Talese rails. Well, well! Is Talese a bit of a right-winger? When I look astonished, he continues: "People only dress up when they're going to a funeral. You should dress for life!" OK, a hedonistic right-winger.

To understand Talese, you just have to stroll through the four stories of this elegant, bohemian building built in 1910, which should become a world historical landmark some day because of all the writers, editors, and journalists who have passed through it. In the huge living room, a portrait of Ronald Reagan hangs next to several photos of the master of the house. An entire shelf of his library is devoted to first editions of Tom Wolfe, along with several of Wolfe's drawings in a somewhat psychedelic style. (Wolfe excels in self-caricature, and his artworks have already fetched staggering prices at auction.) In the basement, which Talese calls "the bunker," there is a large room with a kitchen and bathroom where he retires to write—always by hand, with a Montblanc fountain pen. "I was born in Ocean City, New Jersey, and I came to New York in 1953. I was twenty-one, and I got a job as a copyboy at the *New York Times*. I rented a room on the fourth floor for sixty dollars a month, then, over time, I bought the whole building. That was in 1972, I think." During that time, Gay Talese sublet his pad to William Styron, married an influential editor, and became a star journalist and the author of several bestsellers, including *Honor Thy Father*, the first narrative describing the life of a Mafia family (the Bonanno family) from the inside. "Without that book, I never would have made *The Godfather*," Francis Ford Coppola told me once. "And the producers of *The Sopranos*, the mythic HBO series, have publicly acknowledged what they owe to Talese." At that time, I admit, I had never heard of Gay Talese. Shocked by my ignorance, Coppola started typing on the iPad that never left his side and brought up Talese's bio. With the success of *Honor Thy Father*, Talese became the happy owner of a residence that Tom Wolfe remembers as the site of many wild and glamorous parties: "I came here a lot because it was one of the only places in Manhattan where you could throw parties with a lot, truly a lot, of people." Talese responds, "In his life, Tom has thrown fewer parties than I have but he's written more books."

As for books, Tom Wolfe has published (only) four novels and a dozen nonfiction collections. It's not an exaggeration to say that he writes about whatever is disturbing, about injuries and taboos. In 1968, his first success, *The Electric Kool-Aid Acid Test*, the story of a nutty group of gallivanting hippies on bizarre trips (in both senses of the word), sealed his reputation as a master of literary nonfiction. Then came *The Right Stuff*. And, at age fifty, Wolfe published his first novel, which was brilliant and bitter, *The Bonfire of the Vanities*. That was followed, ten years later, by *A Man in Full*, then *I Am Charlotte Simmons*, and *Back to Blood*.

In his novels as in his nonfiction, Wolfe homes in on whatever goes unsaid and whatever people are afraid to say. As it turns out, these things are often the foundations of America: ambition, sex, the drive to be famous, the arrogance of the powerful, attraction to money, destructive selfishness, the place of athletes in a society obsessed with entertainment, the education of the elite, immigrant communities, racism. He targets self-satisfaction, these famous "vanities" whose shiny surfaces he sets aglow in a giant bonfire. His humor strips as harshly as lye, shedding a different light on these contemporary idols that we worship a bit too easily, whether it's a bestselling author (who turns out to be obsessed with money), an elite black athlete (with a complex about his skin color as much as his small vocabulary), fighter pilots during the Vietnam War or the conquest of space (not so different, after all), multimillionaire traders (without scruples but not without remorse), limousine liberals infatuated with the Left, senior-citizen snowbirds in Florida (who get swindled on expensive contemporary art at Art Basel Miami Beach), or students at elite universities (who smoke joints and have orgies left and right, before devoting their lives to conquering the world). Based on all this, Tom Wolfe constructs mythologies like Roland Barthes—but darker. I ask him about unspoken taboos. "That's where the raw materials of a novel can be found. But also in our daily lives," he says. "I don't look for controversy, despite claims to the contrary. But I refuse to let my thoughts be dictated by a dominant class, whatever it may be. Trends and ideologies make me sick."

What he's interested in, he says, is showing power relations that persist between groups. Could Tom Wolfe have a touch of Marxism in him? He willingly admits it. "I came into contact with Marxism in high school, it's true. But it was reading Max Weber that disturbed me the most: Weber was the first one to introduce the study of social status into sociology." And studying those strategies that we poor mortals use to achieve and keep our position is exactly what captivates Tom Wolfe the most. So, to summarize his recipe: the ideas of Max Weber, but also (let's dig deeper) an old undercurrent of Marxism with, as a bonus, a dash of Balzac, a bit of Zola, a little Dickens, and a pinch of Twain. That's a nice summary of the influences of a writer who likes to sign his letters "Balzola" and who admits that his dream is to one day be considered the secretary of his era, just as Balzac was for his. "America runs on a very special fuel: the huge disparities in social status. That's the source of ambition, greed, revolutions, and everything that upsets us today. Look at Balzac. That's what the whole *Human Comedy* is about: the infinite variety of manners between rich and poor, the ambitious and the social climbers, *nouveaux riches* and losers. America hasn't finished with what was at the heart of the nineteenth century in France. America is a battlefield."

Tom Wolfe has a way with words. This is what led to his incredible success: a high-powered style where catchy phrases are found alongside the most unlikely onomatopoeias, ornamented with ellipses (. . .), exclamation points (!!!), *italics*, phrases in all caps (AHHH . . . !!!), Capitalized Words at Every Opportunity, digressions, and repetitions. "Ornamented?!" protests Tom Wolfe. "Oh, no, not at all, it's not ornamentation or decoration! It's life. The breath of life. The constant fracturing of the stream of consciousness. When I write I'd like to obtain a concert of broken ideas as much as a great spectacle." "And that's what we read," confirms Talese. "Tom Wolfe invented a style. If you want to make a fool of yourself, go try to write like him. In fact, maybe that's what a writer is, isn't it? Someone who invents a style that's impossible to replicate."

It's a style that critics never really understood, accusing Tom Wolfe of writing with a megaphone, thumping his chest, and sticking his finger in an electric socket. Norman Mailer, John Updike, John Irving—though all excellent writers—did not mince words when rebuking Wolfe in hatchet jobs that do them no honor. The prestigious *New Yorker* greeted the publication of Wolfe's books with silence, except for a scathing review of his first novel. "Did that affect you?" Talese asks with concern. "Mosquito bites on a suit of armor," answers Wolfe, who did make the cover of *Time* in 1998 (a rare privilege for an American writer) and whom his (numerous) readers still affectionately call "Mister Wonderful." "It just so happens that a bit earlier I had written some articles that got the goat of all the writers who panned me," Wolfe mentions, with a twinkle in his eye. "Do you think there might be a cause-and-effect relationship?"

Talese interrupts his attack: "But what gave you the idea of writing *like that*?" "I play with words like a child plays with blocks," Wolfe explains. "But since you're asking me about the origins of my style, I'll tell you a story. Do you know about the Serapion brothers?" "No!" Talese says with a start and turns to me: "What about you?" Never heard of them. Wolfe continues, in a soft voice, like a murmur. "The Serapion brothers are actually a group of Soviet writers that no one seems to remember. They wrote about the Russian Revolution, in 1917, in an absolutely incredible way. Their style was very influenced by the French Symbolists, Mallarmé and Baudelaire. They thought that true literature could only be written by madmen, hermits, heretics, dreamers, rebels, and skeptics. They're the ones who inspired me the most, stylistically. I discovered them one night in the Yale library when I was twenty-two, and I clearly remembered saying to myself: 'Oh, if only I could manage to write something like this!'"

Gay Talese's style is less high-octane than Tom Wolfe's, but his projects are just as picaresque. He has not written any novels—only true stories. Each time he had the same goal: to break the laws of silence. This is especially true of his two most successful books, *Honor Thy Father* and *Thy Neighbor's Wife*. To tell the story of one of the families of Cosa Nostra, Talese did not rely on his imagination, as Mario Puzo did in *The Godfather*, but on his doggedness. For five years, he tracked down, contacted, re-contacted, followed, and interviewed Bill Bonanno, the son of one of the most famous New York mafiosi. "I was covering his trial, but he wouldn't say a word in front of the judges. I was only able to get his story because I told his lawyer, 'One day, before he dies in a prison somewhere or in a vendetta, I want this guy to tell me how someone can live being this kind of guy.' And it ended up paying off. One morning, the lawyer called me and said Bill was ready to talk. The condition was that he would tell me his whole life, not leaving anything out, and I could publish the real names. Then I would go check it all." When it came out in 1971, *Honor Thy Father* hit like a bombshell. A journalist who had infiltrated the world of organized crime had obtained confessions that neither the police nor the judges had been able to get. Along the way, he had deconstructed the myth of the Mafia, revealing a human tragedy where existential crises were more powerful than social determinism.

Ten years later, in the early eighties, as the very conservative Reagan years were starting, Talese went even further. This time, he took on Americans' sex lives. From the inside, once again. To research *Thy Neighbor's Wife*, Gay Talese explored all kinds of experiences. When I ask him to talk about them, a tired smile passes over his face. He dismisses the question with a flutter of his hand: "It's all in the book." It is, indeed. Wife-swapping, nudism, infidelity, orgies . . . In order to learn their secrets, he had to win the confidence of these couples, who would reveal their erotic and sexual histories in an avalanche of details. And to do this, there was only one way: "field research" is the euphemistic term Talese uses. What could have been as boring as a long documentary porno turned out to be a virtuoso piece of reporting and the sociological study of a country thirty years after its sexual liberation. A novel, but true. And a huge hit. The movie rights were sold for $6 million. But the critics screamed bloody murder. It's not that easy to go from Puritanism to *Playboy*.

"Field research," "telling the story from the inside," "describing what you saw"—all this sounds like the basics of journalism, you may think. So what did Tom Wolfe and Gay Talese invent that was "new" and made them the founding fathers of "New Journalism," something that is even more fascinating today, when the media settles for producing articles that are ever shorter and ever less informed? "This expression, 'New Journalism,' isn't mine," Wolfe warns. "And while no one can actually tell you whose idea this term was, I can, however, tell you who was the first one to practice it, and that's Gay Talese."

In 1973, Tom Wolfe published his first collection of articles and, while he was at it, designated Gay Talese as the inventor of a new literary genre. The most brilliant representatives of "New Journalism" had been springing up for about ten years in all areas, from criminal investigations to gonzo journalism, along with "participatory athletics." Their names were Truman Capote, Hunter S. Thompson, George Plimpton, Norman Mailer, and Joan Didion, plus Tom Wolfe and Gay Talese, of course. These giants of American literature have nothing in common except that their books look like fiction even though everything they describe is true. "Our shared ambition was to reduce the distance between journalism and literature to the point of confusing them, while remaining factual—without inventing anything," George Plimpton, the iconic editor of the *Paris Review* and another luminary of New York arts and letters, once told me. Tom Wolfe expands on this idea: "We each did our thing, in the territory that interested us the most. 'New Journalism' is most of all about the angle and the circumstances. When I wrote my article on Mohammed Ali, he had no desire to be followed by a journalist for twenty-four hours, despite what he had originally led me to believe. Ali wouldn't speak to me. He didn't answer any of my questions. Then he decided to go for a walk through the streets of New York. So there's the article! Circumstances: the subject you're writing about won't play along but suddenly wants to go for a stroll. Angle: how is the glory of a great boxer expressed on the faces of the people he passes on the street? And there you go, there's your 'New Journalism'–style article."

Talese, the "inventor," wants to make something perfectly clear: "The primary goal of this kind of journalism isn't to inform. Anybody can do that—just look at those robotic men and women who read a teleprompter all day long on TV. Today, you have to work fast and dash off your article, which is also very short. So you can't develop a style. You write slogans. It's not journalism anymore, it's thinly disguised advertising. OK, I'm getting too worked up. The journalism we do is about developing a narrative from true information, that's verified. This requires three things: first, research; then, investigation; and, finally, setting the scene for the story you're telling."

Tom Wolfe's eyes light up as he reaches back into his memory again: "The article that best represents what was called 'New Journalism' dates from 1962. That year, Gay wrote a story about former heavyweight champion Joe Louis. When I read it, it was a shock! There was nothing about his performance, no post-fight interview. It wasn't a portrait of the boxer either. The story started with what Joe Louis and his wife said to each other when she met him on the tarmac in Los Angeles, and it continued with what was going on in Joe Louis's head during his flight back home from New York. How did Gay have the nerve to invent all that? I wondered—before I realized that he didn't invent anything, but he had ridden in the plane with Joe Louis, hearing confessions that he never would have been able to get under other circumstances. That article was a trigger for all of us—Capote, Mailer, and the others. Suddenly, we understood that it wasn't enough to interview someone—you had to live with him. A little bit. A lot. For a long time." Talese accepts the compliment with a nod. "But that's not all," Wolfe continues, in a voice that has dropped to a murmur. "What counts the most is the way the story is told. Gay constructed the scene in the plane, then the scene on the tarmac, the way a novelist would. And, ultimately, this article could easily be mistaken for a short story. That's 'New Journalism': not just a first-person investigation interspersed with statements from interviews, but an aesthetic and literary dimension." So that's how a plane ticket—"bought without an expense account," Talese takes pains to point out—changed the course of journalism.

"Do you want to know the secret?" Talese asks, more impish than professorial. "The fine art of wasting time, that's the secret." Pleased with his effect, he gives a little laugh and refills our glasses. He adjusts his finely striped tie, puts on a quavering but stentorian voice, and improvises an imitation of an old pundit: "Be patient. Persevere. Never give up. Listen a lot. Follow up constantly. Come back later." Wolfe chimes in: "Patience is a prerequisite. But may I add four other points that are essential? First, your story has to be written in scenes that follow each other. Second, include faithfully reproduced dialogue—the *New York Times*, *La Stampa*, *Le Monde*, and newspapers all over the world traditionally ban it, which is absurd. Third, describe each detail when it reveals the social status of the person talking. Fourth, tell what happened from the point of view of your characters, using interior monologue—this way the reader will share all of their feelings and thoughts."

This last point is the most controversial. If I ventured to sprinkle this story with interior monologues by Talese or Wolfe, how could they be true if I invented them? Wolfe explains the practice: "You need to have conducted several thorough interviews, not just brief ones. Four, five, six meetings, over several years, one-on-one, at the office, at home, at the gym, on the street, at friends' homes, at a party, on vacation . . . only on this condition can it be true. Then you will know the person you are writing about so well that you can 'imagine' an interior monologue, and what you imagine will be true. Paradoxical, but effective!" Talese flies to my aid: "The interior monologue is a way of questioning the lure of objectivity, the omnipresence of the 'truth.' But tell me, Tom, when you start 'Radical Chic' with the interior monologue of Leonard Bernstein getting up at 2:00 or 3:00 a.m., walking around his apartment and suddenly having a vision of himself giving a speech against the Vietnam War at Carnegie Hall, how can you know if it's true?" Wolfe answers with a smile: "It's exactly what Bernstein himself described in a biography that's quite hagiographic."

The rest of this tremendously colorful article on Bernstein and his visions triggered a scandal that Manhattan still remembers, making Tom Wolfe notorious. Embedded at a party that the *West Side Story* composer gave for the Black Panthers, Wolfe simply described what he saw: the aristocratic elite of Park Avenue—filmmakers, producers, ad executives, lawyers, judges, TV stars, society columnists, etc.—invited "exotic revolutionaries into their living rooms and thereby achieved the ultimate in Funky Chic interior decoration: live black bodies." The description of Black Panther leaders strolling through this thirteen-room penthouse, among the candelabras and the white servants in uniform offering "little Roquefort cheese morsels rolled in crushed nuts" to ladies of the jet set who raise their fists in their sequined designer dresses is sardonic and hilarious.

"It's the Zola school," Tom Wolfe explains. "I try to express the chaos of life, the chaos of society, and I do it with the hope of creating an effect to astound the reader. I walk in the midst of people who don't know who I am, and I describe. No point in adding anything else. A good, very realistic description is worth a thousand speeches. Journalism has so much to learn from literature: rhythm, but also atmosphere, point of view. We mentioned Balzac and Zola, but let's not forget Hemingway." Talese frowns at this. "Yes, yes, I swear! *The Sun Also Rises* is one of the first works of art that managed not only to capture a certain mental atmosphere in the shape of fiction, but also to turn things around so that they would spread in real life." "Hemingway can't compare to Maupassant," Talese says dismissively. "When I was a kid, we had very few books at home, but my father had brought back a collection of Maupassant's stories from Italy. Then I read the stories of

John Cheever and Scott Fitzgerald. But Maupassant! He's the one who taught me everything about journalism. Sublimely written. And he was interested in ordinary people."

Ordinary people are Talese's choice. Wolfe, when he wasn't writing about the emergence of youth culture or the first silicone breast implants, told stories of celebrities— Cassius Clay and the Rolling Stones, Cary Grant and Andy Warhol, the owner of *Playboy* and the producer of the Beatles. From the beginning, Gay Talese took the opposite tack. He's interested in those who go unnoticed. "If Gay goes to the fights at Madison Square Garden, you can be sure he'll write the portrait of the guy who rings the bell instead of the superstar dancing around on the mat," Tom Wolfe teases, and quickly adds: "But this portrait will not only be something you've never read before, it will also show you the fight better than any TV camera." Doormen, bus drivers, barbers, newspaper sellers, basketball players stuck on the sidelines, an old silent-film starlet fallen into oblivion, the electrician in charge of the news zipper in Times Square, the workers who built the Verrazzano Bridge—these are the people who make up Talese's America. All his talent is devoted to narrating these "minuscule lives." "A newspaper shouldn't limit itself to providing news of society—it should reveal it," he says.

Where does he get this interest in the anonymous, the invisible, the underdogs? "From my parents. My mother had a women's clothing store. As a child, I spent hours in that store and I patiently listened to the conversations: all these ladies told their tragic little stories but no one cared about them. And then, frankly, there was the war." World War II, the big event that silenced many Italian immigrants. Wolfe sits up straight. Talese dives right in: "My father was torn between unconditional support for America, his new country, and love for his two young brothers, who were in Mussolini's army and had been captured by the Allies. Who was going to tell the story of the losers, the brothers who had made the wrong choice? This question literally obsessed me. The losers, the little guys, are also worthy of interest and compassion."

Before we part ways, we talk politics. "Trump, I guess?" Gay Talese asks. "Everyone wants us to talk about Trump, Tom, old boy. And to say what? To say horrible things, I imagine?"

Wolfe and Talese have solid reputations as conservatives. In 2004, being deliberately provocative, Tom Wolfe stated that he was "the only Republican writer in America." When he publicly acknowledged voting for George W. Bush, he was barraged with insults. "It was worse than being called a pedophile," he recalls. "In this country, you cannot be a novelist and vote Republican. Sixty-two million Americans have the right to vote for Bush, but not a novelist. That's how it is. So don't expect me to tell you if I voted for Trump or Clinton," he says with a slightly uneasy sigh. He deplores the two-party system, Republicans versus Democrats. And, even more so, political correctness, whose most insidious form, according to him, is outrage. "Most American intellectuals think you can only be profound if you're outraged. So they're perpetually outraged. It's rather amusing to watch. Wasn't it Marshall McLuhan who said that moral outrage is a common strategy for endowing idiots with dignity?"

That's too good for Talese to pass up. "It's true! It's not like the Dreyfus Affair is happening every day in the United States! And Trump's arrival in the White House is certainly no Dreyfus Affair. But American intellectuals claim to be above this idiotic government and its middle-class voters. They look down on them from the Olympus of their thoughts as if they were worms wiggling around in the mud." "We went through the same thing in the early 2000s with Bush Jr., and before that they made fun of Dwight D. Eisenhower or Ronald Reagan," Wolfe observes. Talese doesn't bat an eye: "It's true that all they did was win World

War II and the Cold War." Wolfe refocuses the discussion: "I'm struck by the weakening of decision-making in America. This collapse is happening at a time when human and financial losses are mounting—war, economic crisis—but above all it's an issue of identity and ethics. Should we be outraged, or should we observe? I prefer the second option by far. A writer isn't there to say what's good or bad. He's there to say what is."

Talese wants to tell a story about Donald Trump that Wolfe says he's forgotten. It was in 1986. They were both members of the PEN American Center, which defends freedom of speech around the world. That year, PEN had invited two hundred writers who had been threatened with death in their home countries. The problem was where to get the money to put them up. "I met Donald Trump at a baseball game at Yankee Stadium and he offered to drive me home in his limo. Some time later, I went to see him and told him about our problem, and you know what? He immediately gave us two hundred hotel rooms in his palatial hotels on Central Park, the St. Moritz and the Essex! Who else could claim to have done as much?" Talese says vehemently. Wolfe replies mischievously: "You said 1986? He sold both those hotels the next year, reaping huge profits. And that's the year when he made a fortune renovating the ice-skating rink in Central Park. Do the outraged tourists who skate around on this rink at Christmas know it's there because of Trump?" Talese scowls, then suddenly becomes animated: "I don't see what's so shocking about making money the way Trump did. Trump talks exactly like thousands of businessmen all over the world. For that matter, you yourself described these kinds of guys in your novels. The traders in *Bonfire of the Vanities* and the hero of *A Man in Full* are like Trump: crude, aggressive, willing to do whatever it takes to get a deal done. So what? New York City was built by people like him. Sure, these guys are con men. But do you think you can build such an enormous city just being swathed in virtue? New York is the result of a history where scams and self-interest dominated virtuous little saints. This city is extraordinary, and it's men like Trump who built it. And because Americans want to have a country that's extraordinary again, they elected one of these men, Donald Trump, as their leader. It's very easy to understand."

Tom Wolfe says nothing at first, then begins to reflect: "It's true, you can easily imagine there's something a little shameful about the way Trump made his money. But in that way, he perfectly represents the American hero. Take Gatsby. Jay Gatsby and Donald Trump could be cousins: we don't really know where they came from or how they got rich, but both are *nouveau riche* thugs who lie about their age and their income, throw parties for people who look down on them or hate them . . . and then there are these women around them." "That's essential, Tom, the women!" Talese exclaims. "If I had to write an article about Donald Trump, I wouldn't tell my memories of him, I wouldn't get into analyzing his politics, I would tell the story of his three wives: Ivana, Marla, Melania. The first one, Ivana, is a former model from Czechoslovakia who managed his casinos. The second one, Marla Maples, is a Southern belle from Georgia for whom he arranged a TV career. The third one, Melania, is also a former model, from Slovenia, and ever since she refused to take her husband's hand when getting off a plane everyone thinks they know her. It's fascinating, right?" Wolfe agrees: "Yes, another story of a meteoric rise and differences in social structure. Ultimately, Trump is really the hero of a novel." Talese adds in a mocking tone: "A novel about an upstart from Queens who's out of control and unpredictable—you've got to admit that it's a lot more exciting than the long novel—eight years!—of a lawyer from Politically Correct College who's raised to the status of a black deity—and therefore impossible to criticize—by a press that itself has graduated from Politically Correct

College. Trump is the face of America. Not the one we want, certainly, but the one we deserve."

The afternoon is coming to a close. With Tom Wolfe's hat in my hands, I leave Park Avenue behind and turn onto East Seventy-Eighth Street, then Madison Avenue. I walk along past the intricate facades, houses of luxurious elegance with plaques indicating the names of their illustrious inhabitants. A few lighted store windows glow in the dusk. I reach Wolfe's building on Seventy-Ninth Street. The sun has plunged behind Central Park and shadows engulf the walls. I stop at the doorway and take a deep breath, inhaling the scents of the evening. The doorman approaches. He's solidly built, with a heavily embellished uniform that looks like something a North Korean general would wear. He receives the white fedora as if it were the shroud of Turin or a relic of the True Cross, then turns on his heels and disappears into the dark marble hallway without a word. Gay Talese has informed Tom Wolfe that I would stop by. Radical, maybe, but chic.

MISS
GULLIVER
IN AMERICA

By
Leïla Slimani

Translated by
Sam Taylor

O n April 16, 2018, New York awakens to a storm. The howling wind strips petals from magnolia trees. Pedestrians walk hunched under pouring rain. That day, I am heading to the *New York Times* to record a podcast about *The Perfect Nanny*, the American edition of my second novel, *Chanson Douce*. In the newspaper's offices on Eighth Avenue, the editors are preparing to crack open the champagne. The *Times* has just won the Pulitzer Prize for its coverage of the Weinstein scandal, a story that has become a global social phenomenon. The fall of the Hollywood mogul was followed by those of dozens of famous stars and, above all, by the rise of the #MeToo movement, which inspired millions of women to reveal the harassment, rape, and sexual assaults that they had suffered. The veil of secrecy was torn away, exposing abuses of power on an unprecedented scale. Women all over the world, from every social class, told their stories. It is probably too early to analyze fully why the movement was born at this precise moment, in a country led by the most misogynistic president in its history. Is Trump's election enough to explain this uprising, or are its causes simultaneously deeper and more extensive? What sparked the #MeToo conflagration, and how will relations between men and women change in its aftermath?

I am on a two-week visit to the United States, giving speeches at universities on the West Coast before publicizing my novel in New York. As I begin writing this essay, I remember Mary McCarthy's mocking nickname for Simone de Beauvoir after the publication of *America Day by Day* in 1948: "Mlle Gulliver en Amérique . . . [descending] from the plane as from a space ship, wearing metaphorical goggles: eager as a little girl to taste the rock-candy delights of this materialistic moon civilization." And yet Simone de Beauvoir acknowledged in her text the immense difficulty involved in understanding a country as complex and contradictory as America. Everywhere I go, people have warned me: "This is not America!" The places that I visit are generally anti-Trump, progressive, and liberal. For most of the people with whom I speak, the #MeToo movement—along with anti-gun protests and Black Lives Matter—is one of the rare hopeful notes in an era that they see as oppressively dark. Patriarchy, guns, and race: three pillars of American society, around which there are increasingly deep and violent divisions.

Marilyn Yalom is a lecturer at Stanford. A resolutely feminist writer and historian, she is filled with enthusiasm when she greets me during my visit. "We are living through a revolutionary moment! This solidarity, this 'me too,' it's absolutely extraordinary. Something is happening between us, between women, that we have never experienced before. We all feel it. The dream of sisterhood, which men have long mocked and considered impossible, is becoming real." Wherever I go, women say the same thing to me. This female unity is regarded as a huge victory. To understand it, one must reread the beginning of Simone de Beauvoir's *The Second Sex*: "Women are not a minority, like the American Negroes or the Jews; there are as many women as men on earth. [. . .] Women do not say 'We.' [. . .] They have no past, no history, no religion of their own; and they have no such solidarity of work and interest as that of the proletariat. [. . .] They live dispersed among the males, attached through residence, housework, economic condition, and social standing to certain men—fathers or husbands—more firmly than they are to other women." So the sisterhood that Marilyn Yalom describes is truly a major historical event. With #MeToo, for the first time, women have the feeling that they constitute a collective force. Topics such as harassment, rape, and the condition of women are no longer buried in small down-page news stories but are blazoned over the front pages of the world's papers. "We talk about it everywhere: over dinner at home, but also in cafés, in libraries, at the office," explains Stephanie, an English major who escorts me around campus.

This is brought home to me during the afternoon that I spend with a group of students at Scripps College in Claremont, California. Founded in 1926 by the wealthy philanthropist Ellen Browning Scripps, this private college was intended to emancipate young women by offering them an education. It now accepts some men, too, and—thanks to a system of scholarships—many students from disadvantaged neighborhoods. When I ask them about the #MeToo movement, these students—all of them pretty shy until that moment—suddenly come to life. For Diane, "it was mostly a chance to discuss these subjects with my parents' generation. For me, it hasn't really changed my relationship with men, but more so with women." It is a thrill for me to see these young women united not only by a feeling of solidarity but also a refusal to accept the old traps of guilt. "Before, when I went home during the holidays, I would go out in baggy clothes, I'd wear a hoodie to avoid attracting attention. Now I feel stronger, less guilty. I no longer feel like it's my fault if someone behaves inappropriately toward me." Zoe, too, is struck by the dialogue between generations: "For the last few months, I've been talking a lot with my mother about feminism, about the patriarchy, about consent. My mother, who had never participated in a protest before in her life, marched against Trump. It's given women the desire to get involved in public life." Only one young man speaks up that afternoon: "The media attention on all those cases of online harassment made me realize that the question of consent is complex," Joshua says nervously. "It makes me wonder how many of my friends have done that. If maybe I've been guilty of it, too . . ."

"This new freedom of speech is fundamental!" thinks Marilyn Yalom. "In my day, we didn't talk about this kind of thing. Nearly twenty years ago, I organized a meeting at the university to discuss violence against women. I was amazed by how many women came to that, from every social background, but who didn't say anything. I remember thinking that I had touched a nerve." Because the story of American women fighting against sexual harassment and violence is not a new one.

In the 1960s, women began to enter the academic and professional worlds en masse. "Back then, women were told that they had to put up with it, that if a man had wandering hands, or worse, it wasn't in their interests to make a fuss about it," says Yalom. At Cornell University in 1975, Carmita Wood quit her job as an administrative assistant after years of being sexually harassed by her boss, a renowned physicist. With the support of a group of activists, she created an organization called Working Women United and launched an event at which female secretaries, filmmakers, factory workers, waitresses, and others could share their experiences. In August of that year, the *New York Times* used the term "sexual harassment" for the first time in an article about Wood. In the 1980s, *Time* magazine covered cases at Yale and Harvard: "At least 18 million American women were sexually harassed at work between 1979 and 1980," wrote the journalist. In the 1990s, at Antioch College in Ohio, female students drew up the first consent policy. At the time, those women were mocked as prudes and killjoys.

And yet, almost twenty years later, their cause seems to have gained ground. Today, consent policies have been adopted by nearly a thousand universities. At each level of a sexual relationship, the person initiating the next step must obtain his or her partner's verbal assent or risk a disciplinary procedure that could lead to expulsion. There are meetings to raise awareness, at which students have to role-play different situations and analyze whether or not the partner has consented. In April 2018, the Yes to Sex app was launched, enabling the interested parties to record voluntary verbal confirmations that are then stored on a secure server that cannot be accessed except in the event of a legal investigation. In this litigious society, sexual relations are judicialized, regarded as risk-laden situations in that everyone involved must—figuratively, if not literally—cover their asses. But the desire to erase all confusion and blurred lines from the realm of seduction seems simultaneously futile and a little terrifying.

Since I've been in the United States, many people have spoken to me about the case of Aziz Ansari, the famous comedian and star of the TV show *Master of None*. In January 2018, on the website babe.net, a pseudonymous woman was the subject of an article about a date with the actor, in which she accused him of forcing her into sexual relations. For Ansari, the relationship was completely consensual, even if he acknowledged having perhaps "misinterpreted the situation." The article proved divisive. What does consent mean? How is it expressed? Is it enough not to say no for the relationship to be considered consensual? What are the foundations of the ethics of consent? In a disturbing short story entitled "Cat Person," which became a viral hit after being published in the *New Yorker*, Kristen Roupenian questions this controversial notion of a "gray zone": after a few dates with a man she doesn't really like that much, a young woman agrees to sleep with him. Is she pressured into this? Does she do it out of a fear of disappointing him? From a fear of confrontation? This murkiness is at the heart of the questions raised by the #MeToo movement.

In France, there is a tendency to dismiss all of this with the hackneyed term "puritanism," a word that irritates every American I meet. Since I've been here, I have also been asked constantly about the infamous open letter signed by Catherine Deneuve and Catherine Millet among others. The defense of the "*liberté d'importuner*"—the idea that a man has the right to make unwanted advances to women—shocked many people here and has been interpreted as irrefutable proof of the profound cultural gulf between our two countries. Where the French signatories see all the life being sucked out of the art of seduction, the women I speak with in America see only a victory for feminism. For them, the verbalization of consent is the best way to prevent rape. "France is an implicit society, where ambiguity is considered an integral part of sexuality," explains Marie Pierre Ulloa, a French academic at Stanford. "Americans, on the other hand, live in an explicit culture. This is particularly striking in the relationships between men and women, and the culture of dating is highly codified. In France, a man will rarely ask you if he can kiss you. In the United States, it's mandatory." Stephanie, the student who guides me around campus, adds: "Here, on the street, you forget that you're a woman. When I went to France, I was struck by the way men looked at me and made remarks, whether welcome or unwelcome. In the United States, public spaces are more desexualized."

It is no coincidence that it is in the universities of America that the question of consent has been debated for almost forty years. In these places, which parents would like to be protected, students were revealed to be living in a veritable jungle of sex, drugs, and alcohol. Rape after rape occurred, often without redress. One young woman confessed to me: "Back when I was at university, I thought of my sexuality as a danger. The day I graduated, I felt relieved. I knew I was going to be leaving campus without having been raped, without having lost my virginity to anyone, and without getting pregnant." Barack Obama himself highlighted the issue of sexual violence on campus, citing the statistic that one American woman in five is sexually assaulted while at university. Only 12 percent of those assaults would be reported, and an even tinier number of assailants would be punished.

The new generation appears to be creating a very different relationship with sexuality, more codified and careful. As we walk the paths around Stanford's campus, the writer Tobias Wolff, author of *This Boy's Life*, points out to me that there is not a single couple kissing or even holding hands: "That's something that has changed a great deal since the 1970s. This new generation of students seems much less romantic. Social networks have played their part in demystifying sex. Students these days spend a lot of time on Tinder and other apps that allow them to hook up for one-night stands."

At the airport in San Francisco, I stop at a bookstore while I wait for my flight to Los Angeles. Most of the magazines have a woman on the cover and feature the word "POWER" as if it were some kind of mantra. Even in the children's section, the books on display glorify female empowerment. Little American girls have a choice between *Strong Is the New Pretty*, *The Little Book of Little Activists*, or *Girling Up*. In Hollywood, I meet screenwriters and producers who are interested in my work as a "feminist writer." In the world capital of cinema, the aftershock of the Weinstein scandal is still being felt. Actresses are on the front lines, battling against rape culture and for equal pay. Producers are careful now to meet with female clients in public places or in the presence of witnesses. But most importantly, for the first time, studios are prepared to invest heavily in screenplays centering on female protagonists: a genuine revolution in this industry that for a long time saw actresses only as arm candy. In the United States, between 2017 and 2018, only 17 percent of leading roles went to women.

It seems to me that the reason the #MeToo movement has provoked such a strong social reaction is that it is in fact the consequence of a slow and profound evolution in American society. It doesn't herald a shift in the balance of power between men and women—it confirms it. As Cécile Alduy, who teaches French at Stanford, points out: "The 2008 economic crisis initially struck real estate and finance, two sectors where men are extremely dominant. In the years that followed, we have seen a significant increase in the number of women who earn more than their husbands." Confronted with Weinstein and Trump—two caricatures of capitalism and virility—women have expressed their determination to overthrow an abusive system. Better educated, better integrated, more financially independent, and increasingly likely to attain the highest positions in whichever field they choose, they are no longer ready to accept the ancient *droit du seigneur*: the lord's "right" to sleep with any woman he wants. #MeToo questions the whole basis of a system that has governed relations between men and women for centuries.

In *Against Our Will: Men, Women and Rape*, published in 1975, Susan Brownmiller asserted that phallic power was based on violence, fear, and the victims' silence: "Man's discovery that his genitalia could serve as a weapon to generate fear must rank as one of the most important discoveries of prehistoric times, along with the use of fire and the first crude stone axe." According to Brownmiller, men's ability to constantly threaten women with rape—in the street, at work, in the home—has given them a means of exercising their power through intimidation and by imposing a form of superiority. But if women are no longer afraid, if they point out that the emperor is not only naked but sexually harassing them, then the entire system must surely crumble.

For Tobias Wolff, Trump's election embodies a profound crisis of virility, the final convulsion of the dying body politic. "American society is sick with misogyny," he says. "Let's not forget the violence with which Hillary Clinton was attacked. People turned a blind eye to it, but she was the object of disgraceful caricatures." Because the truth is that not everybody is happy about this new feminist wave. Many white, heterosexual men have the feeling that they have lost their privileges to the gay, feminist, and black lobbies that they see as conspiring against them.

On April 25, my stay in America is coming to an end. In Toronto, Alek Minassian drives a van into a crowd, killing ten people. Before this, he published a message on Facebook hailing the "incel rebellion." The incels—short for "involuntarily celibate"—are a group of several thousand men in Canada and the United States who blame their sexual frustration on women, whom they regard as "superficial, lying, manipulative and obsessed by appearances." Some of these men are so profoundly misogynistic that they believe rape and even murder are justified. In 2014, Elliot Rodger, a twenty-two-year-old man, killed six people in California after recording a video in which he described his hatred of women and labeled himself the Supreme Gentleman.

For Tobias Wolff, "Trump's vulgarity toward women is considered by many Americans as a form of honesty. Let's not forget that woman who, after 'Time's Up,' wore a T-shirt proclaiming TRUMP CAN GRAB MY PUSSY. Fifty-three percent of white women voted for him!" He reminds me that in 1989, after five black and Latino teenagers, known as the Central Park Five, had been wrongly accused of raping a woman in Central Park, Donald Trump spent $85,000 on a full-page ad in various New York newspapers calling for the return of the death penalty: "I want to hate these muggers and murderers. They should be forced to suffer and, when they kill, they should be executed for their crimes," he wrote at the time. Donald Trump, the defender of women? "Not at all," replies Wolff. "What bothered him was that a white woman should be raped by black men. Rape is bad . . . for black men."

In the United States, the issue of sexual freedom has for a long time been intrinsically linked to race. Black men have been generally stereotyped as hypersexual and violent. For decades they were described as predators, driven by the animal urge to rape white women. How many were lynched for merely daring to look at a white woman? Sexual violence committed by black men was exaggerated while sexual violence committed by white men was minimized, hidden, kept silent. Now, #MeToo has shattered that taboo, showing that rape is a universal problem, connected to the patriarchal system and not to skin color. It would therefore be wrong to regard this movement as simply one small step among others in women's long struggle for their rights and dignity. Its consequences are more far-reaching, involving not only the intimate lives of individuals but politics, economics, and race relations. #MeToo has revealed to us that a new order already exists, even if we still find it hard to perceive: a society where women demand their rightful share of the world.

THE HOME(LESS) OF
THE FREE AND
THE BRAVE

By
Lee Stringer

n December 24, 1985, an elderly woman, a "Jane Doe" known only as "Mama," was roused by a Metro-North police officer from her perch on the benches of Grand Central Terminal's main waiting room. She was well known to the officers, station workers, and dozens of other homeless New Yorkers who routinely took refuge in the huge midtown structure.

She had spent the day quietly, lapsing in and out of sleep, making the rounds every hour or so of the thirty-odd phone booths ranged along the walls, checking the coin returns for an orphan quarter or two. She couldn't do much else. Her legs were profoundly swollen and infected from elephantiasis. She kept them swathed in newspapers, to absorb the discharge from the seeping sores it caused.

At 1:30 a.m. terminal police made their way through the waiting room, rousing sleepers, announcing that the terminal was closing and instructing everyone, Mama included, to vacate the premises.

Outside, it was fourteen degrees below freezing.

With no one to contact, nowhere to go, Mama relocated to an unheated corridor adjacent to the terminal, and spent a fitful night on the cold, heat-sucking, concrete floor. When the terminal reopened four hours later, she returned to the waiting room benches and promptly fell asleep. At 9:30 a.m. she was awakened by police, enforcing the "no sleeping" policy that was in effect at the time.

She opened her eyes, sat up, and for a time stayed awake, but ultimately drifted off again, into a deep sleep. When police returned to wake her three hours later, she was dead.

It was Christmas Day.

When word of her tragic demise hit the six o'clock news that evening, it was sobering information for a public intoxicated by the spoils of the nation's explosive and unprecedented binge of prosperity. Within a week, the story went national. Christmas being the season of human interest in the news game, Mama's sad saga was soon joined by dozens of similar heartbreaking reports from the streets of cities around the nation. By the time the trees had been taken down, and all the high hats and noisemakers had been put away, homelessness had become the number one social issue in America. Early estimates of the number of Americans living in this condition ran from 250,000 on the low side into the millions on the high end. Homelessness, everyone agreed, had reached epidemic proportions.

It was a stunning wake-up call for Regan-era America. *How was it,* everyone wondered, *that smack-dab in the middle of an economic boom, in the richest nation on the face of the Earth, so many people could be so abysmally impoverished?* And to this day, some thirty-five years later, that remains how the homeless issue has primarily been framed: as the neglect of the poor in the face of great wealth and riches.

Despite the numbers that have been crunched and reported—pointing to the fallout of massive tax-cutting, scaled-back social programs, dwindling affordable housing stats, rising inflation, and so on—most persist in seeing homelessness as the consequence of the neglect of the poor by the rich. Few understand, and even fewer are willing to admit, that the uber-poverty that emerged in the heart of our Great Miracle was precisely *how* an elite portion of society got rich in the first place; that the homeless actually represent the billions upon billions of dollars sucked from the very bottom to ultimately enrich the top. It wasn't that all the nouveaux riches had gotten there in some prosperous vacuum and were now being coldly tightfisted toward their lessors.

Reaganomics was a simple proposition: government takes $70–$100 billion less from the public, and that much more money is out there for people to snatch up more goods and services and otherwise conspicuously consume, thereby jump-starting a sluggish economy. A sound and straightforward enough premise, until you take into account who is and isn't empowered in this country, and how that disparity determined where the government trimming to enable the huge tax cuts would come from. As a consequence, the very people who needed the government most—those with the fewest resources and connections—would end up paying the lion's share of the price. At the end of the day, this could only add up to untold numbers of people tumbling to the streets.

Proponents of the tax cuts worked around this fact by suggesting the cuts would simply flush out social-welfare cheats who would then have to go out and get jobs, leaving enough in the till to take care of those truly in need. That was, of course, a lie. At the time, General Accounting Office statistics reflected a less than 2 percent fraud rate in what was then called the welfare system. This could hardly offset the double-digit cuts being imposed.

But people bought it. We are Americans, after all. We were not forged in the gristmill of common history, ethnicity, or experience, like other nations. We were simply founded upon an idea. That idea, and the myths it has spawned about our sense of fairness, freedom, and equality, is all that defines us. Take away our myths and there is no "American" underneath; just a vast heterogeneous populace, all jockeying for purchase on the same terra firma. So, we cling mightily to our myths. Even in the face of all evidence to the contrary.

I can't say I knew Mama. Not to speak to. I knew who she was. I had seen her a few times, there in the waiting room; had watched her do her dogged coin-slot ritual more than once. I was one of what would eventually grow to be two or three hundred people living in Grand Central at the time. Nor can I properly claim to be a victim of devastated social programs.

However, I will not say that my twelve-year bout of homelessness was entirely unrelated to the machinations of the '80s. For that was an era that roundly trounced a supreme longing I'd harbored since I bore the trauma of my third-grade history class. I *hated* that class—despised those downright bestial, gape-nostrilled, saucer-lipped, Currier & Ives etchings of "the negro" that littered the pages of our history primers. I squirmed and burned under the side-eyed scrutiny of my white classmates, drawing parallels between those images and me.

Then there were the history lessons themselves; the courage and valor of the European adventurers on the one hand, and the servitude and lowliness of the African "primitives" on the other. Calculating the math on which of those two peoples' sides I'd rather have been was straightforward enough for an eight-year-old.

Understand: it wasn't a wish to have been born white, exactly—though the divide between the included and the excluded seemed to run firmly along color lines. No, what I wanted was to be counted amongst the free, the empowered, the just, and the enlightened of the world.

What I yearned for, most, was to be an American.

And by the '70s, after much national struggle and strife, I indeed felt a bit more like I was an American; that I was at least part of a place in which the arc of history had been long, as Dr. King had put it, but had bent toward justice.

Then came the '80s. And the cold cunning of a new political philosophy. And along with it the sinking, sickening feeling that the arc was now bending the other way. The premise that now, in order to fulfill your destiny as an American you had to hunger and thirst after the accumulation of wealth, kicked unbearably against something inexorably deep within me. It filled me with a sad, profound resignation.

I did what I did. I made the choices I made. No one forced me to accept that first puff of crack when it was offered. That was all me. No one else is responsible for that. However, I won't say that it wasn't out of my profound spiritual emptiness that I became so immediately and intensely hooked on the stuff. Precarious as it may be to generalize about such things, I think it's fair to say that this much is true of all my contemporaries of the streets: that people fall into homelessness when for one reason or another the lives they are living cease to be viable. I remained out there for over a decade, however—a fact that distinguishes me as being among the so-called "chronically homeless."

There was just such a guy living for years in an alleyway a few doors down from where I once lived, on the Upper West Side. I assumed he had some mental problem, because he never demonstrated any urgency to get off the street. It wasn't until I had been out there a long time myself that I understood.

When I first hit the streets I was in a near panic over how I would eat, where I would sleep, and so forth, wanting nothing more than to scramble back to the familiarity of having my own roof over my own head. But if we humans are nothing else, we are adaptation machines. Before very long I had scoped out the best soup kitchens, established a sleeping niche in Grand Central Terminal's lower level, and spent the rush hours trawling the terminal's multitude of trash receptacles for redeemable bottles and cans.

This averaged me about forty to fifty dollars a day; enough for baseline maintenance of my crack addition. Holidays, when the ranks of travelers swelled, were windfalls.

My take rose to the \$100–\$150 vicinity. A few years later, a publication called *Street News* was launched, the purpose of which was to be bought for a quarter by homeless people and sold to the public for a buck, thereby sparing the seller the indignity of begging for money. The income I made from joining that enterprise beat the can game hands down. Especially when I pitched it to captive crowds on the subway. If an outreach worker had approached me during those days, offering to get me off the streets, I certainly wouldn't have jumped at the chance. That would have involved change, and change always entails loss. If you've fallen into homelessness, you are pretty much loss averse.

In fact, as far as getting *off* the streets goes, it seems to be a habit of our social welfare energy to put things that way: to talk about getting *out* of the ghetto, *out* of Viet Nam, to just say *no* or to *stop* the violence. The thing is, I don't think many people—on the street or otherwise—get all that motivated by a negative. When it comes to changing themselves or their situation, it's not so much a matter of stopping or leaving one thing as it is a matter of starting or moving toward another.

For my part, late one Saturday morning, moneyless, drugless, and with no energy to go hustle up a little cash, I happened to pick up what was part of my drug paraphernalia at the time—a pencil—and applied it to a little boredom-killing. I dug up an old composition book I had, set about writing something about a deathly ill friend of mine.

The next thing I knew, it was evening and I had written and edited a short story. But what astounded me most was that I hadn't once thought of getting high the entire time I was writing. I mean, until then, I couldn't go fifteen minutes without thinking about it.

A few days later, I took the story over to the *Street News* editorial offices, and a few days after that, I opened the new issue, and there was my story. A few weeks later I was

invited to write something else. There was no big money
in it, just a bundle of free papers. But the way they flew
out of my hands, back then, converting them into $100 or
more on the subway took barely an hour.

Eventually I was given a key to the office, so that I
could write on the computer directly. All I had to do then
was keep working until everyone left, and I could crash on
the couch. I wasn't actively seeking to get off the street. It
just happened as a by-product, if you will, of my moving
toward this writing thing.

One day a book publisher by the name of Dan Simon
bought a copy of *Street News* on the subway, liked what he
saw, and called up the publisher, offering to make a dona-
tion or take a subscription.

"And who's this Lee Stringer guy?" he asked at one
point. "I kind of like his writing. It doesn't take me where
I think it's going to go."

When they told me this, I naturally wanted my ego
stroked. So, I called up Mr. Simon, and he invited me to his
office and, one thing after another, I walked out of there
with a book deal and a small (but HUGE for a guy on the
streets) advance of $1,000, which I promptly smoked up
that weekend.

So, there it all was: the thing I was moving toward,
a golden opportunity to get there, and, standing in the
way, threatening to blow the whole deal, was the thing
that had rendered my life nonviable in the first place:
my addiction. I knew full well crack wasn't good for me.
I knew if I kept smoking things would get worse. I knew
full well I wasn't having any fun at it anymore. Yet being
addicted, I just couldn't put that cursed pipe down. Not
by myself, I couldn't.

I knew a guy by the name of George McDonald who,
at the time, ran the Doe Fund (named after Mama, the
"Jane Doe" who had died Christmas Day). I had met him

during the days when he would bring sandwiches to feed everyone in Grand Central Terminal every evening. He had stepped to me one day, while I was selling *Street News* in his Upper East Side neighborhood.

"So, I hear you're on the pipe," he said.

O*h crap*, was my immediate thought, *here comes a lecture* . . .

But he didn't do that, just handed me a twenty and his card. "Well, if you ever want to stop," he said, "please let me help."

Unfortunately, an addict needs to hit a wall and hit it pretty hard before taking that leap. I was no different. It took the bald betrayal of a good friend, and the theft of thousands of her dollars, before my desire to move on from my addiction became more desperate than my craving for the next hit. In the depths of that unwanted darkness, I called George.

I mean, the man said please!

He congratulated me on my decision. Said he was happy to help. Told me to give him three days and call back (because you can't just walk into these programs; you need ID, a case has to be opened, papers have to be filed, etc.). I respected George tremendously, had never once raised my voice to him, but I'm telling you, I screamed into that phone. "I DON'T HAVE THREE DAYS!" I bellowed." I GOTTA GO NOW! IN ANOTHER HOUR I'M GOING TO BE BACK ON THAT GODDAMNED PIPE!"

"Okay," he said, "stay by the phone."

A few minutes later he called back, instructed me to go to what turned out to be a referral center in mid-town, where he had called ahead and vouched for me. They referred me to a shelter/treatment center at 8 East Third Street, which had formerly been the intake center for the city's welfare system and was now occupied by a nonprofit homeless agency named Project Renewal. The people at this agency intrinsically understood homelessness as a symptom and were therefore dedicated to addressing its underlying causes.

I of course did not know this. I only remember walking up the stairs to the facility, *praying* that the people on the other side of the door knew what they were doing. To this day, some twenty-two years later, I remain deeply grateful to everyone working there; right down to the guy who sweeps the floors.

They were there when I had nothing else.

The rest is almost an anticlimax, miraculous as it was. I finished the book. It blew up, was a *New York Times* and *USA Today* top ten pick of the year, went on to publication in eighteen languages. My story was in all the newspapers and on TV, I became friends with the late Kurt Vonnegut. I went to Europe twice to promote the book. I was asked to keynote at the United Nations.

Every now and then I wonder what it was that made the difference. How did my story end the way it did, and someone like Mama's story end as woefully as it did? The best that I can puzzle out is that we are each here to have a personal journey. Take two people, put them in exactly the same circumstances, and you're still talking apples and oranges.

I point to this because I'm often asked what I think the government should do to end homelessness. And since I know of no country in which there are not people struggling at the bottom, I'd have to say that, short of reimagining ourselves, our politics, our priorities—short of America standing up to truly become what it says it is—nothing will help but perhaps upping the budget on what we are already doing.

Homeless people have always been here, albeit in smaller numbers. We used to dismiss them as "bums." The question today is this: What is our relationship to them, person to person? At the heart of this and every social problem lie the fundamental questions: How, in an increasingly textured world, are we to reasonably exist? How are we to remain human to one another?

The answer, I submit, is and has always been that one's humanity is always on-the-job training. You just keep at it. Get up every day and give it one more good college try.

WILL EVANGELICALS
SAVE TRUMP?

By
Philippe Coste

Translated by
Rachael Small

At noon, when the air trembles with heat, a giant shell seems to float above the American horizon. The massive beams that lift the prow five stories high confirm that Noah's Ark is indeed dry-docked on a Kentucky pasture. This ship from Genesis, or rather its five-hundred-foot-long "life-size" copy, has not accidentally run aground on the side of Interstate 75, a half hour from Cincinnati and on the border with Ohio. It's waiting for a flood here on the frontier between the Christian South and the Midwest, where it is regularly assailed by cars full of tourists, and positioned between a jam-packed parking lot and sandwich stands. Its plywood belly resting on concrete columns was not made to sail but rather to drop anchor in people's minds. In 2015 a Christian NGO, Answers in Genesis, spent nearly $102 million, collected through donations and loans, to build this pedagogical monument, which aims to provide the events of the Bible with a Hollywood-like realism. But the enormous boat, named Ark Encounter, is just one branch of a small religious entertainment empire, first begun twenty years ago with the Creation Museum, built forty miles from this spot, in Petersburg, Kentucky. The museum is entirely devoted to refuting Darwin's theory of evolution and reminding people that the world and its inhabitants were created in six days, six thousand years ago.

The founder of Answers in Genesis, Ken Ham, a fundamentalist Christian born in Australia who has lived in the United States since 1989, has not skimped on the details in the Creation Museum, which stages the Garden of Eden as an amusement park. You can even find Adam and Eve splashing around in a pond surrounded by diplodocuses, the highlight of a virtual trip around the world as it existed before original sin—a world where predators graze on grass, where insects and snakes don't bite, and where the life of immortal humans runs on like a long, peaceful river.

For the heretics who would doubt this version of original paradise, the pious curators have also depicted the contemporary alternative. Visitors are invited on a trip across a somber and sordid city, hostile to the heavenly word. As they make their way through murderous alleyways whose walls are stained with newspaper headlines—murdered grandmothers, teenagers engaging in drugs and homosexuality—they can peer in on a young girl plotting her abortion in one window, a boy ordering dope as he plays two video games at once in another, all while their mother cruelly gossips about the neighbors. The message is clear: you'd better follow the Bible, and to the letter!

Every day, nearly one hundred thousand visitors march across the Ark Encounter's vast, meticulously constructed decks, past the bamboo cages where pairs of pre-flood stuffed bears, gazelles, dogs, and wild boars of the highest quality rub shoulders with the dinosaurs that, of course, Noah didn't forget to bring on board. As long as they didn't take up too much space, that is: descriptive panels, ready to banish all doubts, establish that due to the sheer volume of species to be saved, God preferred pairs of young or reasonably sized animals, such as these tiny triceratops or, in their cages on the second floor, those interesting ancestors of the giraffe endowed with very short necks. The enormous menagerie would feed upon bags of grain piled up against the walls; their waste would be discarded using an ingenious elephant-powered wheel, which, as a fascinating interactive animation explains, would chuck it all overboard.

The depiction of the human passengers is also worth going out of your way to see. In wax museum models, Noah, his wife, their three sons, and their sons' wives—one white, another bronze-skinned, and the third explicitly African, three mothers of the earthly races—cut their vegetables or lounge about in djellabas in biblical middle-class show homes, decked out with Pier 1 wicker, wall hangings, rugs, and ebony canopy beds. In the background, Eastern elevator music livens up the scene. A warning posted on the wall reminds visitors that certain "*ark*tistic liberties" had to be taken to depict Noah's clan, such as giving names and races to the patriarch's daughters-in-law, who barely get a mention in Genesis.

"I appreciate that they are open about what they don't know, and that they are professing the truth out loud," David Yonki, a visitor who came from nearby Tennessee with his wife, Magdeline, comments seriously. "In a place like this, I see my faith come to life and become a reality." In a previous life, David was a gas-meter reader in the Bronx. When he retired to the South, this sexagenarian explains, he said goodbye to the rat race of urban life, "its spiritual emptiness, and quite a few personal deviations and struggles." "That's how I decided to go in search of Jesus, and to hand my life over to him," he says.

According to a Pew Research Center report from 2014, despite the rise in atheism and in competing religions, seven out of ten Americans still say they are Christian. Furthermore, among the 173 million believers, a large majority of whom are Protestant, over one third (62 million) say they are Evangelicals, a very diverse contemporary branch born of a series of separations from the main historical churches of the Reformation: Lutheran, Calvinist, and Anglican. While these latter sects practice child baptism, born-again Christians like David mark the renewal of their faith with an adult baptism, during which their pastor, in the presence of their community, immerses them briefly in a basin, symbolizing their spiritual rebirth. Wary of institutional churches, born-again Christians prize spontaneity and a personal relationship to God, and come together for informal and fervent worship, hands raised toward the sky, sometimes in immense fifteen- to twenty thousand–seat megachurches. Whatever their church or denomination, whether their house of worship bears the name Church of Christ, Assembly of God, or the Southern Baptist Convention (the most powerful religious organization in the South), these born-again Christians are God's vanguard. Their beliefs demand missionary activism, and, for the most conservative, the shaping of all of society according to the divine precepts.

Evangelical religious life centers on the Bible. Like all Protestants, Evangelicals see it as the only religious guide and authority, dismissing the tradition of canons and decrees to which Catholics and Orthodox Christians remain attached. Faced with the spread of historical analyses of texts, the most fundamentalist Evangelical movements have reacted by developing a scrupulous, literal reading of the Old Testament. In surveys, four out of ten Americans claim, with at least some conviction, that they are direct descendants of Adam and Eve. More than half are firmly convinced of the existence of heaven and of angels and devils. At Ark Encounter, where entry costs forty-six dollars, these statistics explode. Under the watchful eye of adults, groups of well-behaved children in T-shirts from an Evangelical summer camp move from one exhibit to the next, carrying an entertaining questionnaire that their chaperones dutifully check. According to them, the fact that marine fossils have been found on mountaintops is enough to prove the truth of the Flood. Paleontologists are ridiculed for claiming that they can reconstruct animals based on "little bits of bone." "Boys? How old was Noah when he built his ark?" one of the instructors asks. "Good job, Jeremy: he was six hundred years old. People lived a lot longer back then."

The Flood itself is painted with broad strokes. One scene shows a supplicant society being drowned by giant waves or devoured by sharks. But the crowd spends a long time in the rooms dedicated to the *why*. It's simple: God grew tired of a world ruined by corruption. Grand displays depict, as modestly as possible, the perversions of society before the Flood. Figurines of lascivious women, thighs protruding from their split skirts, sprawl over men on luxurious couches. Others, apparently prostitutes in slinky togas, wait on crowds of clients against backdrops of hybrid urban landscapes of Babylon and American super-cities. "People were nasty," a grandmother tells the four children of a stone-faced couple. "They didn't respect the word of the Lord."

Tourists also search the ark for echoes of contemporary degeneracy. Every night, the vessel is illuminated with the colors of the rainbow. This spectacular kitsch effect reminds visitors that when the Flood was over, God drew this celestial prism as a promise to Noah that he would never flood the world again. "It's time for us to take back our rights to the rainbow," insists Michele Stieve, a soft-spoken fifty-something tourist from faraway Wisconsin. "Young people need to understand that it's the symbol of an agreement with God, not for lesbians and transsexuals."

Around us, in the Ark Encounter's large cafeteria, the atmosphere is reminiscent of Sunday lunches in small towns all over the American heartland. But here we also see additional signs of Evangelical identity. Grandfathers with biblical beards and grannies in dresses with big flowers who have come on church outings share the enormous tables with a polite younger generation: thirty-year-old dads—virile potential patriarchs, many of whom seem to be veritable bodybuilders—whose wives gaze at them adoringly. Nor do these pioneers of traditions and family values scorn political signposting. Along with "Wake Up and Pray" T-shirts, a call to arms aimed at lazy moderate Protestants, insiders decipher codes hidden on T-shirts that display the logo of Chick-Fil-A. This chain of chicken sandwich shops gained national attention in 2012, when the heads of the company spent over $5 million to finance a campaign against gay marriage. Boycotted by the LGBT community, the company and its logo have become symbols of Evangelical resistance to the oppression of "political correctness."

And where does Trump fit into all of this? Among the lunch crowd, there's only one red "Make America Great Again" hat, worn by a five- or six-year-old child. But the president is here with us nonetheless.

Eighty-one percent of Evangelicals voted for Donald Trump in November 2016, endorsing a candidate who, by all signs, should have been condemned to purgatory. Thrice married, known to have bragged about his sexual prowess on the radio, exposed one month before the general elections by an audio recording in which he could be heard claiming that his celebrity allowed him to "grab [women] by the pussy," the president, who has since found himself mired in the scandal of his affair with porn star Stormy Daniels, makes no attempts to prove his fidelity to Christian precepts. The reality TV troublemaker claims to be Presbyterian like his mother, whose Bible he has already brandished. But this is the same man who, with a fixed grin on his face, asked an assembly of pastors to pray that the audience of his show *The Apprentice* would expand when he left NBC. In January 2016, at a church in Iowa, in the middle of the campaign, the candidate almost put money in the Communion plate that was passed to him.

And yet, the banners at the meetings of the Republican Party, with which 56 percent of Evangelicals identify, continue to tell him, "Jesus loves you and Jesus elected you." Donald Trump chose a vice president, Mike Pence, who claims to kneel in prayer multiple times a day, and prides himself on never having a meal alone with a woman, even if she's a colleague, out of respect for his wife. The former governor of Indiana, who signed some of the most restrictive abortion laws in the United States, could be part of the reason for the Christian endorsement, but it's actually the president himself who holds the heart of the Evangelicals. The director of the Independent Network Charismatic (INC), the most active conversion group in America, has compared him to King Cyrus of Persia, the pagan sovereign who allowed the chosen people to go and build their temple in Jerusalem while they were in exile. Paula White, one of the most influential televangelists in the nation, assures her followers that opposing Trump is tantamount to "fighting against the hand of God." As for Franklin Graham, son of Billy Graham, who was revered up to his death as the "pope" of Protestants, he counsels Trump's opponents to offer up prayers of support: "I believe that God's hand intervened Tuesday night to stop the godless, atheistic progressive agenda from taking control of our country," he said about the election itself.

"He's our president," Michele Stieve summarizes, articulating each syllable to better hammer home her message. "But he's not God, huh," adds her husband, Harvey, an agricultural entrepreneur from Wisconsin. "He's just human, a sinner like all of us, who still strives to defend our values." Once more, the couple takes up the refrain of the winners of 2016, which has been repeated over and over in all conversations between Republicans and Democrats, a sign of the country's seemingly irreversible division: "I know how much you must be suffering right now, but we felt the same thing during eight years of Obama." Eight years during which, according to them, the government promoted a permissive and degenerate culture, legalized gay marriage as a stab in the back to the sanctity of family, supported the supremacy of "transsexuals" by prohibiting their discrimination, contributed to what they believe was an explosion of crime rates—which in reality reached a historic record low—and exposed the country to attack by "Muslim terrorists."

So be it. But if they wanted to return America to God, why did they choose the improbable Donald Trump, when five or six candidates in the Republican primaries were defenders of "the Christian nation"? The answer is tucked into American history. God started voting Republican forty-eight years ago, when, despite the success of the social reforms of Kennedy and Johnson, Richard Nixon managed to seduce a working-class electorate—the Catholic workers of the North, the rural Evangelicals of the South—by glorifying their moral values. Reagan perfected this rhetoric, placing America—"the shining city upon a hill"—at the heart of biblical decorum, dedicating his work to the "moral majority," vowing to fight the evil Soviet Empire, that atheist stronghold, and the mullahs of Tehran. But the true revolution took place in 2008. Thrown into a panic by the popularity of his opponent, Barack Obama, candidate John McCain, a centrist Republican, tried to round up the popular Right by choosing as his vice president the governor of Alaska, Sarah Palin.

Athletic and loudmouthed, this daughter of the pioneering masses—a John Wayne in Gap jeans—was the perfect embodiment of the populist rejection of the urban elite. Her literal and unvarnished faith in the Bible, her barely disguised refusal of the theory of evolution, her confidence in the imminent return of Christ, moved conservative Christians to tears. A movement was born, which above all else reflected white America's identity discomfort in the face of its waning cultural dominance, its loss of status in a country that was being governed by a black man, its obsessive fear of feminists, Latinos, the "gay lobby," and the petty dignitaries of Silicon Valley. Religion, a symbol of scorned traditions, allied itself with populism in movements like the Tea Party, which created a platform for these new religious fanatics in Congress. During a trip to Israel, Michele Bachmann, the Republican crusader from Iowa, suggested that her Jewish hosts should convert. And Texas Senator Ted Cruz, the son of a preacher, invited his God full of thunder into the electoral campaign in 2016.

"Trump made short work of his Republican rivals, but he has the political intelligence not to challenge Ted Cruz head on, the Evangelicals' choice," remarked John Fea, a Protestant sociologist from Messiah College in Virginia and author of *Believe Me: The Evangelical Road to Trump*, on the multimillionaire's conversion of Evangelicals. "Trump let Cruz warm up the base. If he came behind him in the primaries among these voters, then Trump knew how to lay down his cards to win the jackpot in the presidential election on November 8." Cruz doubted the loyalty of American Muslims to their country? Trump promised to banish them from the land, even before taking electoral advantage of the massacre at the Bataclan in France and of the shooting in San Bernardino by gunmen affiliated with ISIS. His recovery of American identity, of "a country that will soon be unrecognizable," was not limited to the promise of a wall on the border with Mexico, however. Beginning in 2011, Trump built his reputation in conservative circles and among right-wing Christians by giving voice to the "Birther" conspiracy movement, an extremist marginal group that cultivated racist doubts about the nationality of American enemy "Barack Hussein Obama," to the point where they forced the president to produce his birth certificate on television. And when the winner of the November 2016 elections needed to name a judge to the Supreme Court to fill the position left vacant by the ultra-conservative Antonin Scalia, who had died earlier that year, what did he do? Trump furnished a list of eleven right-wing judges, all willing to outlaw abortion, and granted that his government could "punish" women who terminated their pregnancies. Rather than repelling Evangelical families, for a majority of them, his machismo and vulgar sexism established him as a hero of the threatened patriarchy. As for his brutality, this appeared to them as a guarantee of the sincerity of his promises, while born-again pastors, left to play minor parts in Republican governments, held lengthy debates at conventions about the necessity of having a "strong man" in the White House who would act in the service of their cause.

As comical as his Christian pedigree may be, Trump knew how to weave a web of Evangelical contacts. In September 2015, three months after he announced his candidacy, thirty pastors were invited to his campaign headquarters in New York. For six hours, the pink marble of Trump Tower resonated with prayers and negotiations. The leaders of this religious contingent belong to a group that Trump, who is frequently glued to the television, knows well: preachers of the Prosperity Gospel, a Protestant movement that promises that faith in God can be a source of material success, power, and excellent health, and which gathers together as if by chance the wealthiest televangelists in America. To date, this includes the elite of the INC, a group of entrepreneurs promoting a cultural and spiritual revival through mass media; Gloria and Kenneth Copeland, pastors and authors of twenty books, including the bestseller *From Faith to Faith: A Daily Guide to Victory*; Janice Crouch, beehived diva of California megachurches and ultrarich owner, before her death in 2017, of the Christian production empire Trinity Broadcasting Network (TBN); and, of course, personal spiritual counselor to Donald Trump, the vivacious Paula White.

Pastor of New Destiny Christian Center in Apopka, an Orlando suburb, White did not yet know that she would deliver the prayer at President Trump's inauguration in Washington, on January 20, 2017. But this very blonde fifty-something, revered by her thousands of followers—many

WILL EVANGELICALS SAVE TRUMP?

of them African American—and by millions of viewers of her religious television show *Paula White Today*, was always clear with her public that her meeting with the real estate titan nearly two decades prior "carried the stamp of the Holy Ghost." In 2001, right after the broadcast area of her show was extended to include Palm Beach, where Trump's Mar-a-Lago resort is located, he called to compliment her on her preaching, saying, "You're fantastic, you've got the it-factor." Today, she considers her position as a counselor for Trump to be "an assignment from God." Thrice married herself—today to the rock singer Jonathan Cain, from the band Journey—and criticized at one time by the tabloids for a possible affair with another televangelist, White, who grew up in poverty in a mobile home in Missouri and now has a private jet and a pied-à-terre in New York's Trump Tower, sees Trump as the icon of her prosperity theology. For the multimillionaire, she is a pragmatic guide through the religious mysteries of the Republican party.

Though White dissuaded Trump in 2011 from running against Obama because of bad timing, she gave him the green light at a meeting in 2015 to run against Hillary Clinton, who'd been depicted as the Antichrist for twenty years by the Evangelical media. Five months after this meeting, in January 2016, Trump was finally anointed by the austere patricians of the movement—including Robert Jeffress, the pastor of the enormous First Baptist Church of Dallas, and Jerry Falwell Jr., rector of one of the largest Christian universities in the world, Liberty University, in Lynchburg, Virginia. Interviewed by NPR before the presidential election about his choice of a candidate accused of sexual harassment by sixteen women, Jeffress, the Torquemada of moral values, simply answered, "I want the meanest, toughest SOB I can find to protect this nation."

It's true that Jeffress's plan includes the repeal of legal abortion in the United States. This ultimate goal, the daily obsession of the Christian right for forty-five years, justifies all leniency toward the Head of State's transgressions. The president alone gets to nominate judges to lifetime seats on the Supreme Court, which would then make the repeal of the 1973 Roe v. Wade decision possible. Whether out of conviction or cynical opportunism, Trump quickly demonstrated his determination by choosing the conservative Neil Gorsuch in April 2017. The announcement of the retirement of judge Anthony Kennedy on July 31, 2018, and the choice of his replacement, judge Brett Kavanaugh, confirms a true state of grace for the opponents of abortion rights. Federal judge Kavanaugh supported the government last October, when immigration services blocked access to abortion for an underage illegal immigrant who was being incarcerated. All it would take to pave the way to a durable conservative majority would be for two liberal judges, Ruth Bader Ginsburg and Sonia Sotomayor, to step down during Trump's term.

"[The question of judges] was more critical than any of the other issues that were surrounding the Trump campaign at that time . . . That's the main reason Christian conservatives voted for President Trump," states Jim Daly, president of the Christian group Focus on the Family and one of the members of the White House Evangelical advisory board. The informal assembly, led by Paula White and Robert Jeffress, can rest assured that they have the president's indulgent ear. As of fall 2018, the board included Mike Pence, of course; Jeff Sessions, now the former attorney general and a conservative from a fairly moderate Methodist church; Betsy DeVos, the billionaire secretary of education; Rick Perry, the former governor of Texas and former secretary of energy; Sarah Huckabee Sanders, the former White House press secretary and daughter of former religious presidential candidate Mike Huckabee; and anti-gay secretary of state Mike Pompeo; all claim ties to the Evangelical movement. The voices of the court preachers, representatives of the faithful in the White House, have an equally large influence on foreign policy decisions. The Trump government, usually indifferent to human rights, launched brutal economic sanctions against Turkey in August 2018 to obtain the freedom of Andrew Brunson, an American Evangelical preacher imprisoned at Izmir since 2016 for his alleged participation in the attempted coup against President Recep Tayyip Erdoğan. Three other Americans were subjected to the same fate, but Brunson's particular case touched the pious vice president, Mike Pence, who galvanized the religious right by bringing up his arrest again and again. This was three months before the midterm elections, in which the electoral participation of "Trump Christians" would be decisive.

Other international causes mobilize Evangelicals even more: Israel above all, a nation at the heart of their Evangelical beliefs and prophecies. During the presidential campaign, Trump promised to recognize Jerusalem as the capital of the country in his address to the American Israel Public Affairs Committee (AIPAC), the very conservative pro-Israel lobby. This commitment stirred up divisions in the American Jewish community, which represents 1.9 percent of the population and votes 70 percent Democrat. But the promise was really aimed at Protestants from the South and Midwest, for whom the full and complete restoration of Israel takes place through its capital Jerusalem, the land of Christ's return to Earth at the end of times, and the throne of his forthcoming eternal reign.

Evangelicals don't mess around with this subject. In the southern United States, it's impossible to count all the bumper stickers informing other drivers of an imminent prophesy: "When the Rapture comes, this car will be driverless." On that day, God will take all those who believe in him and bring them to heaven. In the 1950s, the extremely literal imagery of this event showed fathers suddenly rising up above their lawnmowers and housewives lifting off before they could even take their apple pies out of the oven.

The scenario hasn't evolved very much to this day. Those who remain on earth become extras in a disaster movie, in which the devil imposes his dictatorship over the world before the coming of Christ for his millennial reign, a precondition for the Final Judgment, in which the damned fall into a lake of fire, and paradise is established on earth. It's easy to get lost in this tale of divine tribulations and epic battles between creatures of good and creatures of evil, but one point remains precise and tangible: the main part of the prophecy takes place in Israel. The fact that this country is mainly inhabited by non-Christians is a secondary point for Evangelicals since, according to the texts, the Jews will convert en masse during the second coming of Jesus.

So it's no surprise that Donald Trump made sure to bring pastor Robert Jeffress with him on Air Force One to offer a prayer during the opening of the new American embassy in Jerusalem on May 14, 2018. Jeffress, whose sermons have damned Buddhists, Muslims, and Jews to hell, sported a radiant smile in front of Netanyahu.

Yet the crux of the story is more prosaic. On December 6, 2017, Trump decided to announce his recognition of Jerusalem as the capital of Israel—rather than Tel Aviv, long recognized as the capital in accordance with American foreign policy—one week before a decisive electoral deadline: in Alabama, Republican Roy Moore, known for his racism and homophobia, was a candidate in the midterm senatorial elections and was having trouble after the reemergence of accusations of his sexual abuse of minors. Trump, who had conspicuously supported him, was hoping that his announcement about Jerusalem might reduce the abstention rate for Evangelicals, who made up half of the state's population but risked being reasonably disgusted by Moore's actions. Trump had to act, even if it meant upsetting the foundations of American foreign policy in the Middle East. Well, surprise: Jerusalem wasn't able to save Roy Moore from Democratic defeat. And Donald Trump, less than a month after the opening ceremony, signed a waiver delaying the establishment of his ambassador in the very controversial capital—while he waited for the complicated practical details of moving to be sorted out.

Does the devotion of Evangelicals to Republican power—and to Donald Trump—have any limits? The 20 percent of born-again Christians who gave this president the cold shoulder in November 2016 reflect diverse, even opposing, backgrounds, from conservatives outraged by his sexual escapades and his venality to progressives horrified by his social insensitivity, his racist rants, and his authoritarianism. The latter come overwhelmingly from the third of the movement that is non-white and the 19 percent of black people who are frequent megachurch visitors, who are barely less hostile than their white counterparts to abortion and gay marriage, but are worried by the Trump administration's pushback of civil rights.

Their dissidence might have been stifled after the elections, if the new president hadn't very quickly crossed the line. Horrifying scenes at airports during the expulsion of Muslims from the borders in February 2017 pushed nearly five hundred pastors, guided by Evangelicals Max Lucado and Tim Keller, to protest in a full-page ad that appeared in the *Washington Post*. But in April of that same year, the president's scandalously ambiguous statements after the death of an antiracist protester during neo-Nazi demonstrations in Charlottesville, Virginia, and his refusal to unequivocally condemn white supremacists who gathered to prevent the removal of statues of Confederate generals, only elicited irritated throat clearing among the Evangelical elite, and even noisy counterattacks. Franklin Graham went in with a furious diatribe: "Shame on the politicians who are trying to push blame on President Trump," he proclaimed on Facebook. "What about the politicians such as the city council who voted to remove a memorial that had been in place since 1924, regardless of the possible repercussions?"

Silence fell quickly, as it has for each scandal. The Stormy Daniels affair was declared null and void by the same religious mentors who had called for the deposition of Bill Clinton after the Monica Lewinsky scandal.

And yet the forced separation of 2,500 children of illegal immigrants and asylum seekers from their parents, ordained in April 2018 by Trump and his then–attorney general Jeff Sessions, seemed for the very first time to shake the cult of the president. Religious women—in particular educated suburban residents whose votes were at stake in the midterm elections—rebelled against this affront to family values. In one sign of this unease, on June 13, 2018, during a big meeting of the Southern Baptist Convention in Dallas, pastors in the South's largest religious association voted on a resolution demanding reform of the immigration policy to "affirm the value and dignity of immigrants, regardless of their race, religion, ethnicity, culture, national origin, or legal status" that "include[s] an emphasis on securing our borders and providing a pathway to legal status with appropriate restitutionary measures, maintaining the priority of family unity." The motion did not constitute a clear disavowal of Trump, but it revealed, a few hours before Mike Pence's speech at the rostrum, the first political divergences of the Christian assembly with regard to the government.

The White House's emergency communication was aimed, above all, at Evangelicals: "It is very biblical to enforce the law," repeated Sarah Sanders. When she was asked to remember that Jesus, brought by his parents to Egypt to escape the Massacre of the Innocents, was an illegal immigrant, Paula White responded that "it was not illegal. If he had broke the law, then he would have been sinful and he would not have been our Messiah." Jeff Sessions, threatened by six hundred members of his Methodist church who demanded his ouster for the mistreatment of immigrant children, went on the Christian Broadcasting

Network (CBN) to shamelessly lie and swear that "we never really intended to [separate families]." Trump announced the end of child separations. This order sufficed to soothe the conscience of the more sensitive believers. And as for the rest? "Sometimes you have to be harsh to make people respect the law," Harvey Stieve sighs, a pained look on his face and a hand on his heart, before continuing his visit to Noah's Ark.

At the Creation Museum, in Petersburg, we approach Ken Ham, the founder of Answers in Genesis. His blue eyes darken with irritation when he hears questions about migrant families. "And who's talking about the thousands of babies aborted every day?" he strikes back, before returning to the subject. "You know very well that many of these immigrant children are for show, children rented by illegals to soften up the border police," he groans. "Even if they were theirs—what parent would be cruel enough to put their child in that kind of danger?" These remarks, made by one of the most popular speakers at fundamentalist conferences, are pulled directly from ultra-right-wing Internet forums and the most relentless Fox News commentators. They tell us a lot about the Trumpization of Evangelicals, the authority given to the virtuous presidential word on the so-called "fake news" propagated by the mainstream media.

In eighteen months, the president gave eleven interviews on CBN to right-wing patriarch Pat Robertson, founder of Regent University of Virginia. He gave almost as many to Fox News, many more than he gave to other stations. CBN, temple of the family and the Good News, broadcasted a "documentary" in the 2000s that accused the Clintons of murder and drug trafficking, and more recently showed a film, *The Trump Prophecies*, about the prophetic vision of the election of Donald Trump that came to a retired firefighter in Orlando in 2011. The president is at home in this media bubble, whose many black hosts relieve the good conscience of white Evangelical viewers, but also where shock pastor Jerry Falwell explained that 9/11 demonstrated divine anger toward "an America spoiled by homosexuality and abortion," and where no remarks can be made about Muslims without showing a video of ISIS.

At Ark Encounter and at the Creation Museum, even the Disney Channel is deemed suspect by the in-house lecturers, since it propagates this "twaddle about the birth of Earth billions of years ago." What do they say about the classic media? The Ark shows visitors two videos on a loop. One of them shows Noah answering questions from a preflood journalist with a tattooed face and a posh fake English accent, who is mocking his boat-building project. The patriarch, good common sense incarnate, answers him point by point in a candid tone reminiscent of Columbo, while the thunder of the Flood rumbles in the distance. In another docudrama, a cynical and vulgar reporter is sent from New York to make fun of believers. She returns transformed and serene, assured of her salvation at the end of times after meeting Ken Ham.

The hatred of mainstream media, a Trumpian specialty, resonates most clearly in statements and sermons that perpetuate a siege mentality. Robert Jeffress went on Fox News to argue for parallels between Evangelical Christians today and Jews during Nazi Germany: "I want to remind people that the Nazis weren't able to take the Jews to the crematoriums immediately. The German people wouldn't have allowed for it. Instead, the Nazis had to change public opinion. They marginalized the Jewish people, disparaged them, and made them objects of contempt . . . [Christians] are being marginalized right now, treated as objects of contempt by the media. And once that happens, then the taking away of further rights will be very easy." At New Life Church in Mount Vernon, Paula White, her arms lifted, eyes closed in ecstasy, finishes her sermon with a more positive exhortation: "You can't change a culture dominated by Hollywood and the media," she proclaims. "You have to create an entirely different one."

On June 22, on her way to Washington, the Floridian televangelist makes a stop in New York to, among other things, grace with her presence a seminar on Christian leadership in a black church on the faded borders of the Bronx. "God created you in his image. He sees you in all your triumphs and your achievements," she shouts, rattling off a couple Bible verses at the crowd of pastors and humble neighborhood residents. "It's up to you to lift yourselves up to his expectations." What follows is a retelling of her own Stations of the Cross: the poor little girl, sexual abuse victim and teen mother, who found the light and Donald Trump, "a man who, by the grace of God, can change the world." The church's Ghanaian pastor politely waits for the star to leave in a procession of limousines before he addresses the audience: "One of our followers was arrested by ICE and has been in prison for six months, even though his papers were in order," he says. "I know that many of you are worried. But Mrs. Paula White will be at the White House tomorrow. She tells me that she will speak to the president."

BOULEVARD OF BROKEN DREAMS

By
Yann Perreau

Translated by
Emma Ramadan

t's one of the first scenes of *La La Land,* Damien Chazelle's 2016 musical: Mia, the young ingenue played by Emma Stone, smiles at the customers from behind the counter of a coffee shop while she thinks about her audition later that afternoon. Anyone who lives in Los Angeles has probably found themselves in a similar situation when speaking to a waitress or bartender. If you strike up a conversation, the majority of them will tell you that they do this job "on the side" as they wait to land the role that will at last reveal their unjustly overlooked talent.

The "City of Angels" has always worked this way, like a sort of gigantic phantasmagoria attracting thousands of people from all over the world who come each year to "pursue their dream," which is to say, most often, to work in film, television, or video games: the "entertainment industry." "Handsome queer boys who had come to Hollywood to be cowboys walked around, wetting their eyebrows with hincty fingertip. The most beautiful little gone gals in the world cut by in slacks; they came to be starlets; they ended up in drive-ins," Jack Kerouac wrote. How many have succeeded? How many have found themselves stuck outside the gates instead?

At the end of 2010, I went to research the American Dream in the town where it is manufactured. The book that resulted from my peregrinations, *California Dreaming,* is comprised of portraits of immigrants who came to try their luck in Southern California. I was especially interested in the Hollywood "gofers," those who carry out the thankless jobs peripherally related to their passion: a Belgian bodybuilder lending his biceps to various studios and still dreaming, at forty years old, of becoming the next Arnold Schwarzenegger; "Malibu Joe," a Senegalese paparazzo who has befriended some of the people he photographs; or Diego Alione, a Mexican actor celebrated in his home country, who has been turned into "Rambo in flesh and bone" at the Hollywood Wax Museum. They all assured me that they were living their American Dream—albeit in different ways from what they had originally imagined.

Seven years later, I thought of them again as I watched the election of Donald Trump. What would become of them, those more or less legal residents living on the margins of the system, hoping one day to find a role in it? Would they still believe in the American Dream a few years from now or would they give up and go back home? I remember the night of the election like it was yesterday: We were in the home of Randal Kleiser, the director of *Grease* and *Blue Lagoon*. There were about fifteen people, including a number of foreigners working in "the industry," as they say. The person sitting next to me on the couch had a lump in his throat. An actor from the Netherlands, N. had overstayed his visa. Threatened with deportation, he hadn't driven in months for fear of being stopped by the police. After an unsuccessful green card marriage, he would end up going back to Europe, definitively burying his dreams of Hollywood glory.

Business as usual, many will say regarding Trump. Notoriously pro-Democrat, Tinseltown has naturally produced a number of films critical of those in power; for example, in the wake of Watergate, the New Hollywood of the 1970s, led by Francis Ford Coppola, Dennis Hopper, Brian De Palma, and Martin Scorsese, produced its famous paranoid thrillers, such as *All the President's Men* and *Easy Rider*. Trump's election is actually a good thing for Hollywood, according to Charles H. Rivkin, president of the Motion Picture Association of America (MPAA), the highly powerful trade association that represents the biggest Hollywood studios. In a 2018 feature in the *New York Times*, Rivkin claims that "President Trump probably knows this industry better than any president since Reagan." Like Trump, Reagan has a star on Hollywood Boulevard, having begun his career as an actor in Westerns. "I think [Trump] understands that entertainment is important both as an economic force—jobs in every single state—and as a projection of American values." A former diplomat and Ambassador to France from 2009 to 2013, Rivkin knows what he's talking about: cinema, along with weapons, has always been a lucrative export for the United States.

"*'AMERICA'* / always means two things," Wim Wenders states in his 1984 prose poem/essay "The American Dream":

> a country, geographically, the USA,
> and an idea of that country, the ideal that goes with it.
> . . .
> No other country in the world has sold itself so much
> and sent its images, its SELF-image
> with such power into every corner of the world.
> For seventy or eighty years, since the existence of cinema,
> American films—or better, this ONE American film—
> has been preaching the dream
> of the unexampled, exemplary,
> Promised Land.

In Washington, however, as soon as the president-elect came to power, he published Executive Order 13769, or the "Muslim Ban," as it would come to be called, "to protect the Nation from terrorist activities by foreign nationals admitted to the United States." Sixty thousand people were prohibited from entering America that winter because of their country of origin. At the eighty-ninth Academy

Awards ceremony, for the first time in decades, the winner of Best Foreign Language Film was not present to receive his award. Refusing to go to the United States, the Iranian filmmaker Asghar Farhadi sent a message from Tehran "out of respect for the people of my country and those of the other six nations who have been disrespected by the inhumane law that bans entry of immigrants to the U.S." United Talent Agency, which represents the filmmaker, cancelled its traditional Oscars party to express "the creative community's growing concern with anti-immigrant sentiment in the United States." The agency announced that it would donate $250,000 to the American Civil Liberties Union and the International Rescue Committee.

Still in effect today, the "Muslim Ban" has undeniably tarnished the American Dream, and those who construct it. Last winter, two filmmakers invited to the Sundance Film Festival, the Franco-Syrian Soudade Kaadan and the Iranian Arman Fayyaz Mojtahedi, were denied visas. Over the phone, their American lawyer explained the sad banality of their case: the request was made at their countries' consulates as usual, but the passports were sent back without any form of explanation.

Ironically, Hollywood was created in large part by the European immigrants who found freedom in America when their home countries were sinking into fascism: Ernst Lubitsch, Billy Wilder, Fritz Lang. So how should we sell this "great film that is America" when the president who is supposed to incarnate it is one of the most detestable men on the planet? If the American Dream signifies, as historian James Truslow Adams defined it in 1931, "a dream of a social order in which each man and each woman shall be able to attain to the fullest stature of which they are innately capable, and be recognized by others for what they are, regardless of the fortuitous circumstances of birth or position," is this really true of Hollywood?

"The dream still exists." This is the first response actors, managers, producers, and technicians give. Who would dare claim the contrary? Optimism is a form of patriotism in America, where the "pursuit of happiness" is an inalienable right, like liberty or equality. "If the American Dream is the ideal according to which everyone can achieve what they hope to accomplish one day, I would say that today, Hollywood is closer than ever," David Rabinowitz insists. Cowriter with Charlie Wachtel of the film *BlacKkKlansman*, Rabinowitz retraces the steps of their success story and its happy ending: writing the script along with a friend from college, sending it to a producer, attracting Spike Lee's interest, the success of the film upon its release in 2018, being awarded the Oscar for Best Adapted Screenplay last winter. A story in which two relatively unknown people from New Jersey became two of the most acclaimed screenwriters in Hollywood. The true story of a black cop who infiltrated the heart of the Ku Klux Klan, *BlacKkKlansman* also evokes a dark chapter in the history of American film studios, when the "American dream factory" served the reactionary ideology of those in power. The movie opens with the filming of a televised message of racist propaganda, an explicit reference to the 1915 film *The Birth of a Nation*, by D. W. Griffith, which embodied America and its eternal values for a long time, and which Spike Lee has denounced vehemently throughout his career.

"Hollywood is sort of like a cruise ship making a turn," Charlie Wachtel suggests: "It's taking a long time, but it seems like it's starting to make progress." As a consequence of the Time's Up and Black Lives Matter movements, the industry can take pride today in a phase of increased equal opportunity, one of the foundations of the American Dream. Although the statistics still leave much to be desired—women counted for barely 27 percent of those employed in various film industry jobs in 2017, and only 4 percent of directors of the most popular films of 2018—minorities are certainly better represented than in the past, as exemplified by the trio of Mexican filmmakers Alfonso Cuarón, Guillermo del Toro, and Alejandro González Iñárritu, who have been consistently recognized in the last five years at the Golden Globes and the Academy Awards, or by Barry Jenkins, who was awarded the Oscar for Best Picture in 2017 as the director of *Moonlight*, the story of a young homosexual African-American man, or by Mahershala Ali, who won the Oscar for Best Supporting Actor in the same film.

John F. Kennedy once wrote of the American Dream that it was "in large part the product of millions of plain people beginning a new life in the conviction that life could indeed be better, and each new wave of immigration rekindled the dream." With her practice of about one hundred lawyers of fifty different nationalities, Lorraine D'Alessio helps thousands of actors with the immigration process in California each year: "When it comes to Hollywood, I can tell you that I have more and more requests each year, especially from Canada, China, Australia, and Europe." She specifies the types of jobs her current candidates are applying for: acting in movies and television, of course, but also in the video game field, and the novel profession she calls "influencing"; it amuses her to have to "educate the federal authorities" about marketing, social media, and the new digital economy. D'Alessio admits having encountered a few difficulties under the Trump administration, notably linked to the decision to drastically decrease the number of H-1B visas given out for "specialty workers." So other solutions must be found, such as applying for an O-1 visa, granted to those with "extraordinary ability in the sciences, arts, education, business, or athletics." The immigration process in the United States is long and complex, with many hurdles to overcome before attaining a green card, which, after five years of living in the US, opens the door to American citizenship.

"Of course the American Dream exists!" proclaims Roxane Mesquida, who meets me in a hip café in West Hollywood. The French actress hopes soon to obtain her American citizenship, having lived in the country for ten years now. With her sulky pout and her long eyelashes falling over her big blue eyes, she possesses the beauty of a young Romy Schneider, her role model, to whom she's been compared since adolescence. She explains that she decided to immigrate to the United States "on a whim," after being insulted in the Paris metro by a mother who had not appreciated her provocative role in the 2001 Franco-Italian film *Fat Girl*, directed by Catherine Breillat. "In France, they said to me: you're crazy, you have to be famous before you can have a career in Hollywood." However, everything happened "like in a fairy tale," she says, smiling: her first apartment, "where Charlie Chaplin once lived, if we're to believe the landlord"; her roles in the films of Gregg Araki, Quentin Dupieux, and Xan Cassavetes, and in the series *Gossip Girl*. She specifies nevertheless that none of it would have been possible without her manager and his contacts: "In Hollywood, you don't get hired without an introduction or a godfather," she warns. "It's sort of like a family." A family—or maybe a mafia. The very exclusive Hollywood club gravitates around six big agencies—the Big Six—outside of which it's difficult to forge a career: Creative Artists Agency (CAA), International Creative Management (ICM Partners), Endeavor (formerly known as William Morris Endeavor or WME), United Talent Agency (UTA), Agency for the Performing Arts (APA), and Paradigm Talent Agency.

Criticized for their stranglehold on the system, and currently in a power struggle with the Writers Guild of America (WGA) union, these agencies are no less formidable scouts of talent abroad. Some managers also play this role, such as Eryn Brown, who roams film festivals the world over, looking for rare pearls. That's how she discovered Günes Sensoy, the lead in Deniz Gamze Ergüven's film *Mustang*, nominated for an Oscar in 2016. The young teenager from Turkey confesses to having cried every day of her first year in Hollywood over the friends whom she missed, but also admits having felt immediately "at home": "As if all this," she says, gesturing at the palm trees, the pool, everything around us at the Hollywood Roosevelt, the hotel we're meeting in, "as if all this had always been a part of my life." She is delighted that she's been accepted at the University of California, Santa Barbara, where she will get her degree in psychology, with a minor in film studies. However, a certain sadness is perceptible in Günes's eyes, perhaps because she still has not landed a major role three years after her arrival in Los Angeles.

On this sunny March morning, Hollywood does in fact look like a boulevard of lost illusions. Blonde wig, crimson lips, white dress, and a beauty spot on her cheek, "Marilyn Monroe" is seated on the pavement, staring into space. The tourists ignore her and her plastic bottle cut in two, extended for dollars. They prefer the imitation Jules Winnfield, the gangster played by Samuel L. Jackson in *Pulp Fiction*, with his impeccable black suit and afro wig, who a bit farther on is delivering that famous mishmash of Biblical citations, now entered in the annals of film history. "So, once more: / the 'American Dream,' what does it mean?" Wim Wenders was already asking himself in 1984. "Too many people had to pay for it / and not only at the box office." At the intersection of Hollywood Boulevard and Highland Avenue, the subway unleashes a crowd of tourists into La La Land. The expression signifies, in today's language, a pipe dream. It's also the name of the biggest souvenir shop in the neighborhood, where one can buy figurines made in China to look like Oscar statuettes, "for the best sister in the world," "the best dad," and so on. Farther on, one of the most popular stars on the legendary

Walk of Fame, if we are to believe the official website, is that of Donald Trump. It is regularly vandalized, to such an extent that the West Hollywood city council is currently trying to have it removed, an act to which the city council of Hollywood remains categorically opposed on principle.

"Hollyweird" is also the birthplace of the Church of Scientology, which owns eight of the most beautiful historic buildings in the neighborhood, including the L. Ron Hubbard Life Exhibition, the museum dedicated to the life and work of Scientology's founder, and the Celebrity Centre, a kind of gigantic Bavarian castle on Franklin Avenue. The neighborhood, occupied by the film industry since the early 1900s, today resembles a sort of giant theme park, invaded by mass tourism and freaks of all kinds. Its big studios— Paramount, Universal—left in the 1980s to set up offices on the other side of the hills, in the Valley. Dream or nightmare: how many actors have washed up here, working in the porn industry because they weren't able to convince anyone of their talent on the right side of the hills?

Élodie Bouchez, who lived in Los Angeles for a long time, recalls her agent who, over the years, ended all their meetings with the same line: "Are you ready to become a star?" However, not everyone is trying to become a celebrity or make it in Hollywood. Ali Abbasi has always told his American agent, who contacted him after his first big break, that he didn't have an American dream, but instead "a European dream of cinema." This Danish filmmaker, born in Tehran, is also the exception who confirms the rule: he managed, at the last minute, to slip through the cracks of the "Muslim Ban" to present his film *Border* at the Telluride Film Festival. He describes the months of negotiations, the dozens of lawyers, the lobbying on the part of his manager, the contacts at the highest level of the Trump administration and even in the Senate, all the necessary efforts to get around the ban. "I expected it, because I had already been to the United States twice and been treated like a serial killer: interrogations at the border, et cetera. But not to this extent!" Although he hasn't closed the door on the idea of one day shooting a film in the United States, he does not understand those who, after their first ounce of success, pack their bags to go live on the other side of the Atlantic. "The idea of the Hollywood dream, if you take it seriously, will frustrate you," he explains. I discussed this with David Lynch, and we agreed on the right way to think about this dream: as if it were a fable. Of course *Mulholland Drive* comes to mind, the best film ever made about Los Angeles according to numerous critics, starring Naomi Watts as a young, manic ingenue on a mission to conquer Hollywood.

    The American film industry loves nothing more than stories that propagate its own fantasies, especially films depicting actors, singers, and cinema or music hall starlets, such as *The Artist*, by Michel Hazanavicius, or *La Vie en Rose*, by Olivier Dahan, two of the most recent French films to receive Oscars. The third remake of the 1937 film *A Star is Born* reminds us in 2018 to what extent the Hollywood dream is still, and always has been, the dream of becoming a star. This is the secret desire of the young singer, played by Lady Gaga, whose fame will surpass that of her partner, played by the film's director Bradley Cooper, whose own desires are thwarted as he grows increasingly jealous of his protégée. One scene shows them looking out at the city from a balcony at Chateau Marmont, the famous hotel on the Sunset Strip. Cooper asks Gaga to close her eyes: he wants to surprise her. When she opens them again, she's facing a gigantic billboard erected in her honor, her face bigger than the snowy mountains in the distance. The story will end tragically, of course: the Hollywood moral seems to suggest that we can dream of glory, but we have to pay the price. Marilyn Monroe, Veronica Lake, the Black Dahlia. "Hollywood Babylon," as Kenneth Anger calls it. Not to mention the gruesome fate of Sharon Tate, actress and wife of Roman Polanski, killed by Charles Manson in their Hollywood Hills home in 1968, the backdrop for the new Quentin Tarantino film, *Once Upon a Time . . . in Hollywood.*

"You're searching for the Hollywood dream? Come see me at my office," suggests James C. Katz, a renowned producer who's worked with many of the greats, including Billy Wilder and Clint Eastwood. "The Lot, Writers Bldg., Suite 313," his card indicates, an address at the intersection of North Formosa Avenue and Santa Monica Boulevard. One of those rare historic buildings still dedicated to its original use: cinema. Technicians can be seen mounting a set. "Hollywood is a brand first and foremost," the producer emphasizes. "Nostalgia has always been part of its history, its mythology." Although the "dream factory" continuously recycles yesterday's old formulas, proliferating remakes in all genres—Tim Burton's *Dumbo* in 2019, a new *West Side Story* from Steven Spielberg planned for 2020—Katz prefers originals to copies. He was one of the pioneers of the restoration project launched in 1980 by Universal Pictures Classic Division, thanks to which we can watch the masterpieces of Alfred Hitchcock, Billy Wilder, and John Huston today in optimal conditions.

"Like a dream I remember from an easier time," reads a gigantic fresco painted recently above the arches at Windward Circle in Venice Beach, a few yards from the ocean. It's a reference to the famous opening scene from *Touch of Evil,* in which Charlton Heston and Janet Leigh cross the US-Mexico border on foot. Sixty years ago, the same arches served as the backdrop for the shooting of the 1958 Orson Welles film. The neighborhood is not host to many film shoots today, nor, for that matter, to many artists, filmmakers, or poets. Rent has become prohibitively expensive since Google set up its offices here. As for the murals, through which marginalized communities formerly expressed their demands and dreams for a better life—as Agnès Varda depicted in her 1982 film, the very beautiful *Mur Murs*—the majority of them have completely disappeared, erased by real estate developers or replaced by advertisements. On the former home of Anjelica Huston, a mural promotes season two of *Killing Eve*, the BBC America series: blood drips from above Sandra Oh and Jodie Comer, "Sorry Baby" scrawled across them in hot pink handwriting.

"Hollywood is kind of over," says a regretful Bret Easton Ellis, seated in one of his regular haunts, the restaurant Musso & Frank, a place Bukowski and Bogart also frequented. "The Hollywood of tomorrow is Disney, is Marvel. The historic studios are losing steam, they do more and more movies and fewer and fewer films." It's the reign of franchises, *Star Wars*, *Transformers*, *Avengers*, and company, whose merchandise now brings in more money than ticket sales do.

Sean Penn shares the same opinion: "Is the American Dream still relevant? If you're talking about the idea of coming here to be liked and assimilated, I don't believe in that at all." The actor-director keeps as far away as possible from Hollywood. When he's not busy surfing or investigating the disappearance of the Saudi journalist Jamal Khashoggi in Istanbul, he shuts himself in his Malibu home to devote himself to literature. His first novel, *Bob Honey Who Just Do Stuff*, published in 2018 in the United States, is dark and full of black humor, in the vein of Charles Bukowski, Penn's friend and mentor, of whom a gigantic portrait hangs in his living room. *Bob Honey* tells the story of a paranoid America, in which a septic tank salesman wanders in search of meaning in his life. "It's kind of the *mise en abyme* of the American Dream, if you like. The idea that, if you push the dream to its end, you will find yourself in a sort of civil war." A sentence in the book sums up this idea: "America, it seems to Bob, is no longer that beautiful girl who'd birthed him. But instead, the ghost of a girl he'd never known." Penn describes the culture in his country, which he believes is becoming "more and more egotistical, individualist, mercantile." He compares it to an iTunes library, "those catalogs where anyone can go pick out what they want without paying attention to what his neighbor is looking at. We could also see it in an optimistic way, because it allows for democratization." He celebrates the success, thanks to Netflix, of Alfonso Cuarón's *Roma*, "which—no matter what you think of it—at least sells us something other than the same old-school macho hero. A film in black and white, made by a Mexican director."

2018 was also the year that two Hollywood block-busters, in addition to *Roma*, took an interest in distant countries. The first superhero film ever nominated for an Oscar, Ryan Coogler's *Black Panther* takes place in an imag-inary African country, while Jon M. Chu's *Crazy Rich Asians*, filmed primarily in Singapore with many Asian-American actors, was a box office smash. Criticized for being more and more isolationist, is Trump-era America in the process of opening itself to the rest of the world through its films?

David Ng of the *Los Angeles Times* puts things in per-spective, commenting that ten years ago, the film indus-try made the majority of its profits domestically, but the reverse is true today, with 70 percent of its income now made abroad—in Asia, Europe, and the Middle East. The journalist describes the changes in an industry guided by exports as much on the symbolic level as in the global economy. All those superhero films, produced in succession by the big studios—Marvel, Sony, Paramount, Universal—were made with Chinese and Indian audiences in mind. A report by his newspaper describes this year's "event": the premiere in China of the latest in the Avengers series, *Endgame*, which made $100 million on opening day there.

Los Angeles, end of September 2018, California Sci-ence Center: Hulu, the video streaming service, launches to great fanfare the premier of its new series, *The First*, a saga in the vein of *The Right Stuff* about the mission to Mars. In his speech, the showrunner, Beau Willimon—the creator of *House of Cards*—references a childhood dream, kindled when he saw Neil Armstrong walk on the Moon. The series pilot is screened, for the first and only time, on a big screen, and the audience is invited to a reception in a gigantic hangar where Endeavor, the space shuttle that garnered NASA so much glory, is on display. A Hulu executive talks about the shows currently in production, notably the highly anticipated third season of *The Handmaid's Tale*. Recipient of numerous awards at the Golden Globes and the Emmys, the dystopian series inspired by the Margaret Atwood novel is the engine that allows the new video streaming service to boast 25 million subscribers. How does the American Dream of today play out in the writers' rooms of these television series? David Ng cites the fact that television today represents 80 percent of Hollywood productions, versus barely 20 percent for traditional films. He points to Netflix, the platform that Damien Chazelle and Martin Scorsese have turned to for their next feature films, where there is more wiggle room and more creative freedom than with a traditional studio because of the resources at their disposal. He also notes that these platforms are not under any pressure to fill theaters, so they can take more risks.

We must also look to Northern California, to Silicon Valley, to understand what the future has in store for Hollywood. All the members of FAANG (Facebook, Apple, Amazon, Netflix, Google) are currently invested in producing content, such as television series or games. As in an episode of *Black Mirror*, will we soon have to turn on our cell phones to connect to the American Dream? "That's already the case," argues Randal Kleiser, "but maybe in the not too distant future you'll need an Oculus Rift VR headset to plunge in." The director spent the last five years filming season one of *Defrost*, the first series to be shot entirely in virtual reality. Filmed in 360 degrees with a brand-new kind of camera, *Defrost* invites the viewer to participate in the adventure unfurling before his or her eyes.

American distributors were too timid, so it's a Chinese company, VeeR, which specializes in the new VR technology, that allowed Kleiser to bring his idea to fruition. From behind the computer screen in his Runyon Canyon office, he inaugurated the global launch of *Defrost* on April 27, 2019, via a live stream in Beijing.

I think back to Malibu Joe, my Senegalese paparazzo friend. He was able to resolve his situation recently thanks to the efforts of a Lebanese lawyer "who knows how to work the system," as Joe describes him. A small miracle for an individual who's overstayed his visa for years. Married and the father of two American children, he is currently writing a script for a feature film based on his experience. It was the idea of a producer close to one of the actors Joe befriended when photographing him. "America is magical, my brother," Joe smiles. "Sky is the limit, as they say here." The American Dream still has a bright future ahead.

WE MUST
FIGHT FOR
OUR MEMORY

An Interview with
Louise Erdrich

Conducted by
Julien Bisson

JB   *What does the term* Indian *mean to you?*

LE   It's complicated by the historicism of that term: India is where Columbus thought he was going, and *American Indian* became a term of choice for over a century, until the '70s. I still use the terms *American Indian, Native American,* and *indigenous* really interchangeably, but I like *indigenous* best. I think eventually we will get to a point of calling each person by their tribal identity, instead of having this one overarching word. So I'd be Ojibwe, Turtle Mountain Ojibwe, or Chippewa, and somebody else would be Navajo and they would have their clan name. There are a lot of identity markers that haven't really been used as specifically as I would hope, but it's beginning to happen with writing.

JB   *Is the Native American world unified, or are there divisions between different nations?*

LE   Every tribe has a different history and a different relationship with the US government. I wouldn't say that there are deep divisions; there's a sense of unity of purpose to protect Native American rights and treaty rights. Whether you are an Apache from the South or an Iroquois from the North, there's a feeling of commonality and fraternity, symbolized by the National Museum of the American Indian in Washington, DC. This museum is the symbol of another fight, that of the repatriation of Native American artifacts and sacred objects under the Native

Graves Protection and Repatriation Act, which says tribal people have the right to take back sacred objects from museums. We demand our history back. And because the term *Native American* is based on a legal definition, that is the reason why there are so many Native lawyers. We recognize how important law is to our survival. Becoming a lawyer is much more important than becoming a writer, for instance! Treaties are the legal underpinning of the existence of the stronghold of reservations and reservation land, and those are strongholds of culture and strongholds of identity.

JB   *Why's that?*

LE   In Ojibwe, *ishkonigan* means reservation—the left-over land, as in the leftovers, the remains, the scraps after a meal. Those pieces of the meal are still tremendously important, and these homelands are the strongholds of religion and culture. They are where our ancestors are buried. They are the meeting grounds. This is where people go when they say, "I am going home." But *ishkonigan* is said in some bitterness, because these lands are only tiny fractions of those guaranteed by treaties. Today, huge energy interests are successfully bribing tribal councils to push their plans through illegally and to lead the new manifest destiny. And this manifest destiny has an ugly end that will affect the entire world.

JB   *Is* colonization *the right word to describe what happened and is still happening today in the United States?*

LE   Yes. To be colonized is to have your identity erased. It is to have your culture, religion, forms of worship and dress, and, crucially, your language erased. It is to give up your land and the wealth of that land. It is to be pressed into the service of a more powerful nation. All of those things are still happening.

JB   *How and where does the Native American stand in the American popular culture today?*

LE   I don't like that savagery and violence are so often associated with Native American people. When Bin Laden was killed, it was called *Operation Geronimo*. That was heartbreaking, considering that Native men and women have served in the military and served in World War II in higher numbers per capita than any other group of people and have always been there for the United States. As is commonly known, various teams in the NFL—the Redskins, the Braves—use racist terms and logos.

At Standing Rock, I think that was one of the most difficult stereotypes that people had to overcome. Protesters were portrayed as savage and frightening and ready to riot at a moment's notice, which was utterly untrue. That protest was based on spirituality and a spiritual relationship with the Earth. An increasing number of people are terrified of climate change and willing to wage peaceful protest because they know this pipeline is a "fuse to death." The prophecy is that the "black snake"—i.e., the oil pipeline—will destroy the world.

JB   *What progress has been made in the United States for the indigenous communities since the 1970s?*

LE   Incredible progress! First, I would mention the 1978 Religious Freedom Act. Obviously, this is a country based on religious freedom. The "American Dream" really is to have this freedom, and yet Native American people were not allowed to practice their own religions without consequences from authorities like the Bureau of Indian Affairs, or even the local police. So since then, religious ceremonies have flourished, and people have rediscovered what it means to have religious freedom. American Indian culture is tied up with religion and spirituality, so this has been a great renaissance for people. The respect for Native belief systems is very important because when Christian missionaries came into contact with Native people, they felt the people had a void of spirituality, when in fact Native culture is based on a very deep relationship with the Earth, the land, the universe, everything in one extraordinary web of life. It's a very different outlook from the Christian idea that all of the Earth is there to be conquered, destroyed, used up, and taken, that human beings can do whatever they want to the Earth without repercussion. There's a very great respect for the mysterious entity that is our world. Our place is humble; it's not to be the destroyer of worlds, but to give whatever life we can to respecting our place in the world.

The Indian Child Welfare Act stopped the theft of children by state social workers, who scooped them up to be adopted into non-Indian families. The Native American Graves Protection and Repatriation Act compelled museums to return the bones of our ancestors, the sacred pipes, drums, scrolls, and other items vital to Native religions.

Another mark of progress is the "Tribal College Movement," which situates colleges on tribal land. It's an incredible asset for people living on reservations to be able to get college education there. I have to put casinos in an ambivalent category because they've brought some evils but also, by and large, they have given Native Americans lots of power. Economic power is what speaks to the government. And in many cases that money has been used very wisely. I have to say I've been impressed with the Mille Lacs Ojibwe, who have used the money to sponsor and strengthen their Ojibwe culture.

JB   *After all this progress, what is left to be achieved? What would you hope for in the next ten to twenty years?*

LE   In spite of these great positive surges, there are many issues that still remain. The statistics are still painful. Native Americans experience the highest rate of suicide

and incarceration per capita, poverty, extraordinary violence toward women. One in three women are victims of
rape. So my hope is that the judicial systems on reservations will be strengthened so that non-Indians who com-
mit crimes on reservations can be prosecuted. I also have
great hopes for the traditional foods movement. Native
people eating a Western diet high in sugar and saturated
fat and processed carbs like white flour suffer extremely
high rates of diabetes. Traditional healthy foods, such as
wild rice, venison, bison, wild herbs, greens, and berries,
are making a culinary comeback.

Those are just a few things. It's the same with Native
education. We have the lowest number of high school
graduates. I think that one of the biggest efforts is to get
people—and that's part of why my bookstore, Birchbark
Books, is here—to concentrate on literacy. It's a fact: the
more books you have in your house, the more successful
your child is. That's what I believe in. We have to have books
that speak to Native people and to young Native people.

JB   *What movements are being led to maintain and protect
indigenous culture today?*

LE   One of the most important movements in the
Native world today is the indigenous language movement.
There are 566 different Native American tribes, and some
have entirely lost their language. I'm very proud because
my daughter is an Ojibwe-language teacher at an Ojibwe
immersion school. An immersion school is one way of trying
to bring children from a very young age, when their brains
are like sponges, into the knowledge of the language.

JB   *Is folklorization a threat to Native American culture?*

LE   *Folklore* and *mythology* are colonialist terms for our
systems of awareness. We call our stories *teachings*. In the
case of the Ojibwe, we have our own star maps, our own
mathematics, our own enormous medicinal history and

knowledge of the pharmacopeia of the swamps and forests and woodlands. This knowledge is often encapsulated in teaching stories, but these stories are also there to amuse. Many of them are very funny. American Indians have a sense of humor in common, particularly because our stories always have a trickster god, who does absolutely amoral and idiotic and very funny things. Creation stems from the trickster god.

JB *The majority of indigenous people now live in big cities. How does this fact contribute to the evolution of Native American identity or identities?*

LE The US government has always wanted to erase indigenous identity and seize tribal land. In that way, things haven't changed so much. During the 1950s, instead of supporting tribal infrastructure on tribal land, instead of creating jobs where people actually lived, the government put money into programs that would draw off enterprising young people to urban areas. They were called "areas of economic opportunity," but those areas could just as well have been on reservations, thus strengthening traditional families and culture.

Ojibwe culture has always been dynamic, has always taken from other cultures what it needs or wants and discarded other parts of the culture that are unnecessary. What is not probably visible is the continual back and forth between reservation and city. City life more and more incorporates this; there are calendars full of powwows and gatherings and language classes and all sorts of ways to live out your culture.

JB *How should Indian culture be preserved in modern America?*

LE Native culture has nothing to do with Western culture in its essence. I can guarantee you that very few Native people are totally acculturated, because our culture is based on a completely non-Western culture. But one must also understand that this meeting of cultures is historically recent. Minneapolis was Dakota land. The streets are Dakota. This area right here was the planting ground and cornfields of the Dakota people. This is in recent memory, not in archaeological memory. There are photographs of people who lived here, who hunted here. I hired two young women at the bookstore, and it turned out that their ancestry led back to the exact land on which the bookstore is built, Dakota land. Cloudman's Village was the name of this area. Cloudman's people were the undisputed owners of this entire area, and so these two young women had literally come home.

I am lucky because I knew my great grandfather. My great grandfather was in the last buffalo hunts; he hunted buffalos all through Montana and finally came back into North Dakota. He lived through this vast, vast change. My grandfather knew all the things my great grandfather knew and spoke the language. We all have these very radically connected histories, radically connected to this land.

JB   *How do you react when Donald Trump makes fun of the massacre at Wounded Knee in his tweets?*

LE   At Wounded Knee, women and children in the bitterest cold were gunned down and buried in a mass grave by members of the United States military. Trump is viciously ignorant. What he represents is a willed amnesia, an active cruelty. He's both a terrible mistake, and the embodiment of all that is wrong with our country. But he is not alone in this forgetting. History is so often written as though Native people have never existed, as though America was "discovered" by white people. It's very troubling to me that accurate history is so invisible. I think this is changing, and I'm encouraged by the insistence with which black Americans are talking about the legacy of slavery. It's up to us to fight for our memory.

JB   *What is the role of artists in this fight?*

LE   I'm excited because there is an enormous surge of powerful writing. The poets are coming forth with such energy. Natalie Diaz; Layli Long Soldier; my sister, Heid Erdrich; and our United States poet laureate, Joy Harjo. When you look at countries that are being threatened with fascism, where democracy is under siege, like the United States, this is a time when people look to the poets. In ordinary times, poets are an essential, but not towering presence. Those are times as usual, when we are stumbling along in democracy. At this hour, however, it is the poets whom everyone needs, and everyone is reading. Our poetry is right in front at the bookstore because people need poetry. They need the immediacy of poetry. Poets can evoke the spirit of the times, can give utterance to our fears with essential image. Poetry readings foster the sense of freedom and community. Poetry has become perhaps the most important form of expression.

JB   *Why haven't there been major films or television series on Native American life and history?*

LE   There are major films, and also television series, like *Northern Exposure*. The must-see films include *Powwow Highway*, *The Fast Runner*, *Smoke Signals*, and *Kanehsatake: 270 Years of Resistance*, by legendary Abenaki filmmaker Alanis Obomsawin. There are indigenous world movies like *Whale Rider* and *Once Were Warriors*. Also, Maori director Taika Waititi is making marvelous movies. *Hunt for the Wilderpeople* and *Jojo Rabbit* are my favorites. In the early '90s, there were some successful films, like *Dances with Wolves* and *The Last of the Mohicans*, but these were White Savior films. It isn't easy for non-Indians to make films about Native people. The problem is one of being truly open, of trying to see past stereotypes. The depth of complexity of hundreds of different tribes and hundreds of different languages, the legacy of historical trauma but also the resilience—all of this figures into a work. The one non-Indian-directed big-budget movie I still like is *Little Big Man*, starring Dustin Hoffman. It had a sense of humor, and aside from Dustin Hoffman some great Native actors like Chief Dan George. That's just a few—it's time to get started on your own indigenous film festival.

JB   *Is there a reticence to deal with the national guilt of this history?*

LE   Absolutely. Our country has trouble leaving behind the heroic settler narrative. But there is no denying that Native people have been murdered and exploited through-out history, and into the present. One of the foundational series of books most American children read are the *Little House on the Prairie* books. I began to write the *Birchbark House* series in order to show what life was like for Ojibwe people during the settler conquest, and how the Ojibwe were (and are) warm-hearted and resourceful people. We have our own stories to tell about those times.

JB   *What are the challenges that young Native Americans will face in the coming years?*

LE   I think the challenge will be the same for every-one: the climate crisis. This is particularly true for Native Americans. In Navajo country, in Mohave country, where their water has already been stolen and diverted to Phoe-nix, to Los Angeles. I am reading a stunning collection of poetry by Natalie Diaz called *Postcolonial Love Poem*. She has written powerfully of water, of her people's language and water, and of the harnessed Colorado River.

Standing Rock was about the fact that the Dakota have an amazing water source that could be defiled in a moment if the pipeline, which runs beneath, were to leak. These tremendous pieces of climate chaos are definitely going to affect people in cities and on reservations. Climate change will suck down our economy. There will be fewer and fewer jobs, unless we come to terms with the fact that we have to change very quickly.

The Green New Deal is very exciting, and I think that could really bring back the energy for young people, because included in the Green New Deal is a push to make our economic system work for all people, not just those at the top end of corporations. We have dismantled the regulations that worked to keep our economy stable, and we have to restore those regulations. The inequity in our financial system and the amount of debt that young people labor under here are so profound. At some point there's going to have to be a reckoning. There was never a golden age in American history for everyone. There was a golden age for wealthy white males, but if you were working class or black, Hispanic, or Native, or a woman without access to birth control, there was not a golden age.

I like to think that there will be a golden age, however, one where there's a stable climate, a steady state economy, a place where you can pursue your happiness without being saddled by vast amounts of debt, where you're not being sucked in by desperation and drugs, where you're not trying to make a living and failing at it while your parents were at least able to make ends meet. We need a new vision for the world based on clean energy. If the United States—still the world's largest economy, and responsible for half the world's carbon emissions—can come to terms with our climate reality, we could bring forth a Green Golden Age for everyone.

AMONG THE
AMISH

By
Philippe Claudel

Translated by
John Cullen

He might have been playing dead. Lying on his left side, his head resting on the asphalt, the wind ruffling the ringed fur of his tail and belly. The thin, rounded claws at the ends of his paws were folded in on themselves. His wide-open eyes pierced his black mask, staring at a mossy embankment in the distance. Three drops of scarlet blood had formed on his black snout; they reminded me of rowanberries. The sun poured a dusty light over him, like pinches of dry, gilded, sparkly earth filtering down through foliage. He was the first raccoon I'd ever seen. I'd swerved to avoid his body as I came around the bend, and a little farther on, I'd parked the old Chevrolet Impala a university colleague had loaned me.

Squatting on my haunches, I gazed at the animal. A teddy bear with a gamy smell. A cartoonish beauty. Unreal and sweet. All of a sudden, the theme song from *Daniel Boone*, a television series I never missed a single episode of when I was a kid, came back to me. I'd sing the French version of the opening verse at the top of my voice while roaming the Lorraine countryside, an adventurer in my daydreams:

> *Daniel Boone was a man,*
> *Yes, a big man!*
> *With an eye like an eagle*
> *And as tall as a mountain was he!*

Fess Parker, the actor in the leading role, wore a cap made of a raccoon skin, much like the coonskin cap he'd already worn in another TV series, *Davy Crockett*, where he'd also played the lead. The animal's ringed tail hung down the back of the actor's neck, and the little beast's face sat atop his forehead. The show took place at the end of the eighteenth century and was very freely based on the life of the Kentucky pioneer, whom the American creative spirit incorporated into its great factory for producing legends.

A sound of horse's hooves brought me back to reality. From around the bend in the road, a two-wheeled buggy appeared: long, thin shafts, high wheels, black, faded hood, the contraption drawn by a horse whose nostrils were covered with flies. Inside the buggy, an Amish couple. The man, around fifty years old, had a broad-brimmed straw hat and a long red beard. Dressed in a black vest, a pair of black trousers, and a gray, collarless shirt, he was a head taller than his wife. Her face disappeared almost entirely beneath a white cotton bonnet, which was tied under her chin with a ribbon. She kept her hands placed flat on the skirt of her long, puffy, blue denim dress, at the hem of which appeared the round tips of two muddy boots.

I raised my hand in greeting. The man replied to my salutation with a movement of his chin while simultaneously giving the horse a light tap with his whip. The woman showed no reaction and kept looking straight ahead. The blue of her eyes was very bright, almost unsettling. The frail carriage, pulled by the trotting horse, moved off into the luminous checkerboard of the forest and then disappeared.

I had arrived in Pennsylvania three weeks earlier, invited by Indiana University of Pennsylvania (IUP), whose main campus is in Indiana, Pennsylvania, to give a seminar on French literature and culture. Located an hour from Pittsburgh, the town had a population of just under twenty-five

thousand, including IUP students. Straight streets, shaded
by sycamore maples; attractive houses behind well-
maintained lawns; a mall; a movie theater; three supermarkets; one store licensed to sell alcohol, including wine; and
a few other businesses. A tranquil, verdant, placid corner
of America, barely disturbed on weekends by the raucous
drunken binges of certain students, who would eventually
pass out under the cedars in the little public park.

The town was the birthplace, in 1908, of James Stew-
art, later the star of films directed by (among others) Frank
Capra, Ernst Lubitsch, and Alfred Hitchcock, in addition
to being a war hero. He was one of my favorite actors, and
I never tired of seeing *The Shop Around the Corner* or *It's
a Wonderful Life* yet again. A little museum on the third
floor of the Indiana Country Community Building paid
tribute to him.

Indiana, Pennsylvania, had another famous son, even
though every time I mentioned his name, I sensed a certain
embarrassment among the people I was speaking to, who
didn't dare confess they'd never heard of him: Edward
Abbey. He was even the reason I'd accepted the invitation
from IUP. I wanted to know the place where the author of
Fire on the Mountain and *The Monkey Wrench Gang* had grown
up. Abbey was one of the great nature writers. He died in
Tucson, Arizona, in 1989 and was buried somewhere—no
one knows exactly where—in the Sonoran Desert.

I was lodging with a couple of septuagenarians, Ed
and Mary. Their Victorian-style house reminded me of the
one in *Lady and the Tramp*. Mary had been born here in
Indiana, where her mother was a teacher and her father a
hardware dealer. Ed was originally from suburban Dallas,
in Texas, and had been an actor in Hollywood. A B-list
career, mostly in westerns, at a time when the genre was
dying out. Some framed photographs showed a dusty Ed,
his Colt .45s strapped to his hips, alongside Clint Eastwood, Ernest Borgnine, or Yul Brynner. A square-jawed

giant almost six and a half feet tall. Fists as big as bowling balls. Dazzling smile.

Mary looked like a vole. Some fierce chemotherapy had made all her hair fall out. She wore a dark-brown wig. My preference for light breakfasts drove her to despair, and she never understood why I didn't want the bacon, the pancakes, the green beans with tomatoes, the slices of buttered toast, and the omelets she prepared for me each morning. She had a nice smile. Ed often laid his hand on her shoulder. The two of them stood on their front steps and watched me leave every day, as if I were the son they'd never been able to have. I'd lower the driver's window on my borrowed Chevrolet and say goodbye.

My students' ignorance of everything that had to do with the European continent—where the majority of their ancestors had come from—never ceased to surprise me. On the first day, one of them asked me if all the homes in France had electricity and running water. Another wanted to know the name of my country's current king. One of his comrades asked what language was spoken there.

Most of the students lived on campus and came to class in their pajamas, especially the girls, who wore matching sets in pink terrycloth or flannel decorated with patterns of bees and butterflies, and on their feet, slippers of the same color, adorned with tufts of synthetic fur. They would hold enormous lattes, which they'd sip over the course of an hour, all the while eating doughnuts and fritters that would leave shiny, greasy spots on their lips. Many of them yawned. Some slept or kept their eyes closed for so long that I couldn't deceive myself into thinking they were actually making a determined effort to concentrate on my lecture. By the end of class, the room smelled like fried food, sour coffee, bodies massaged by the night, sluggish exhalations. The students would exit the room slowly, like a group of horses leaving the stable when the weather outside isn't conducive to grazing. I'd had to scale back my expectations;

the classes I'd prepared were too complex. The first one ("At the Roots of Autobiographical Fiction: The Proustian Enterprise") had left my students in a state of stupefaction approaching catatonia. I settled for sketching a panoramic summary of the chief modern artistic currents, citing some of the best-known names, reading some extracts from the classics, and projecting reproductions onto the wall, mostly photographs of paintings that had traveled around the world in the form of placemats and designs on neckties, toilet lids, and ashtrays.

One day, however, I began class by saying, "This morning I want to speak about Monet," and the reaction that statement elicited gave me a false hope of interesting my students at last. The majority of them suddenly arose from their torpor and for the first time raised their eyes to look at me. Others suspended their morning mastications and smiled openly. Galvanized by all that new attention, I went on: "Yes, I want to speak about Monet this morning!" and joyful exclamations burst out, even accompanied by applause, which I was able to stifle with a somewhat exaggerated hand gesture, though at bottom, I was happy to have awakened such enthusiasm.

I was aware that Impressionism was incontestably the art movement that Americans knew best and appreciated most, and that Monet represented for them the quintessence of art, but I hadn't thought that the mere mention of his name would suffice to arouse my young audience.

The first reproduction of the *Water Lilies* that I projected onto the wall had the effect of a cold shower. Smiles disappeared. Eyes widened. Jaws sagged. I heard an increasingly loud sound that was filled with disappointment. I pretended not to notice anything was wrong and introduced the work, remarking as an afterthought intended to impress my listeners that the finest paintings in Monet's extensive *Water Lilies* series were in New York, in the collection at the Museum of Modern Art. I was interrupted by the atrociously nasal voice of a student dressed in a shapeless tracksuit. She looked like a somewhat skinnier Mariah Carey.

"Excuse me," she said, "but you told us that you wanted to talk about money! Where's money in this colored shit?"

The misunderstanding was now clear to me. I wrote on the blackboard, "Monet is not money." Speaking aloud, I added that Monet was the name of the painter. A famous painter. At this point, part of the class realized that I wasn't going to be talking about money and left the room. The others went back to sleep or finished their breakfasts, consulting their telephones the whole time.

I remained alone with the *Water Lilies*.

I gave classes only in the morning. I'd spend the rest of the day driving around the countryside, slowly, with the windows down. The weather was fine. I rediscovered the rural smells I've always loved.

It was on one of these excursions that I'd come around a bend in the road and seen for the first time, in a field a hundred meters away, an Amish family. Father, mother, and children, nine or ten of them, boys and girls, ranging in age from adolescents to toddlers, as well as a newborn still in its mother's arms. They were all moving forward in a line. Those old enough to do so were reaping the grain with a hand sickle, and when they had a sufficiently large bundle of stalks in their arms, they'd bind them with a few barley stems and place the sheaves on the ground behind them.

Beyond all this activity stood the forest, composed of tall, leafy trees barely shaken by the late afternoon breeze. In the sky, the sun, already low, took on a slightly reddish hue. No words could be heard. Gestures were made in the most absolute silence. The whole company was mute, and even though I was some distance from them, I could distinguish their facial features, which expressed neither joy, nor sorrow, nor trouble. Nothing.

The girls and their mother were identically dressed: white cotton bonnet, tied under the chin and protruding at the top and sides, hiding their cheeks. Big, dark-blue dress that reached down to their feet. Gray smock tied over the dress. The hats the father and sons wore all had the same shape, with broad, circular brims, but some were straw hats while others seemed to be made of felt. All the males had on the same kind of baggy, shapeless trousers, held up by suspenders worn over a light-colored long-sleeved shirt. At the edge of the field, two horses were posing like statues. Unmoving, their heads lowered, standing beside a big cart already partly loaded with sheaves.

I had a sensation of skidding, as if space and time had suddenly hiccupped in concert. Without any warning, I was projected into a world that until then had existed for me only in the edifying works of painters dead and buried for more than a century and a half, or in some of the realist novels that were written by the hundreds throughout the course of the nineteenth century. A few kilometers from where I was standing were human beings who couldn't live without their cell phones clutched in their hands, who ceaselessly checked computer screens, who moved around in air-conditioned vehicles with over-sized engines and wheels, who listened to music that penetrated their brains through wires as thin as hairs, who ate processed, frozen food that they heated in microwave ovens, who flopped down in front of televisions to watch a recorded baseball game, a comedy show enhanced by canned laughter, or the interminable, hackneyed loops of so-called information, the racket of the world, broadcast continuously by the news channels. In this collage of two universes so distant from each other, there was not only the exoticism of an inexpensive change of scene, offered to all those who, like me, were willing to look, but, also and above all, food for thought about existence and its choices.

America is often mocked because of its desire for absolute sovereignty, its exportation of an ultra-free-market,
consumerist economic model, its unnuanced apprehension of the complexity of the world, of civilizations, and
of humankind, its lack of an appetite for culture in all its
forms, preferring emollient entertainment for immediate
use. Yet it is also the country that tolerates the margins
when they offer no frontal challenge to the national ethos
and the nationally accepted modus vivendi. Within the general framework, many groups can live very different lives,
following choices that a number of European countries,
starting with France, couldn't legally tolerate.

At six in the evening that day, some colleagues had organized a party in honor of my arrival. I was going to stay
for only four weeks, but as a foreigner, I represented an
event to be celebrated in the little town, where basically
nothing much happened, except for the serene flow of the
course of things.

There were about thirty of us, drinking California
Shiraz and picking at plates of colorless, tasteless cheese
cut into little cubes. The house was spacious, one-story,
opening onto a lawn surrounded by a hornbeam hedge and
some copper beeches. A flagpole planted in the middle of
the yard was flying an American flag.

Near a big fireplace in which some electric logs were
turning red, two fifty-somethings with guitars were playing
tunes by Bob Dylan, Neil Young, and Joni Mitchell. Inevitably, they had attracted a circle of four or five women their
age, who joined in the choruses of the songs and looked
at the performers with loving eyes. The phenomenon was
the same as when I was seventeen. On either side of the
Atlantic, the guitar remained a sure means of attracting
girls, but I had never been persistent enough to reach the
point where I could play well, and as a result, my sex life
had begun rather late.

I shook various hands and answered various questions. All the people I talked to smiled at me. The thick, sweet wine was very drinkable, and the atmosphere was cordial. Most of the guests were Americans, but a few French people had slipped in among them, expatriates of such long standing that they were no longer sure which country was theirs. They looked at me with a hint of nostalgia in their eyes and spoke to me in our mother tongue, which they pronounced with a slight accent, occasionally straining to remember this or that word.

I sensed in them a will to convince themselves that the life they had here was fulfilling beyond all comparison with the lives they would have led had they stayed in France. The United States was the land of limitless possibilities. The proof: Jean-Patrick, PhD and agrégé, a professor of history, and a specialist in motte-and-bailey castles and siege architecture in the High Middle Ages, had radically changed tracks at the age of forty-six and become a gardener, the creator of immense vegetable gardens on the outskirts of Indiana, plots of land in which he toiled alone from dawn to dusk, trying to grow tomatoes, pumpkins, beans, potatoes, and peas according to strictly natural and biodynamic standards, with limited success. As for his wife, Nelly, an American, a professor of English literature who had done her thesis on inter-rhythmic prosody in Christopher Marlowe, she had resigned her position at Harvard to take up the artisanal production of cow's-milk cheeses. The little cubes—that was her.

The two of them had the thinness of devotees and the ardent eyes of pioneers. Later, when I paid Jean-Patrick a visit and saw him, alone with his hoe in the midst of a field several acres in area, locked in dogged battle with the invading brambles and weeds, he made me think of Marcel Pagnol's poor Jean de Florette. Under a sort of arbor he'd built himself out of hazelnut branches, his body sweaty and gnarled, his hands red with blisters and calluses, he insisted on my tasting an abominable pear brandy of his own concoction, all the while extolling the richness of the soil from which a few starved-looking tomato plants were emerging.

Another colleague, Mo, who on my first day had spontaneously offered to lend me a car—"Don't worry, there are only two of us, but we have four cars"—talked to me about her husband, who had left his job as director of a pharmaceutical laboratory in Pittsburgh two years earlier in order to pursue his passion for theater. Since that time, he'd been crisscrossing the country in a bus bought for the purpose with the members of the theater company he'd created, The Rolling Voices. The group performed plays of his own composition, dealing with civil and minority rights, before enthralled audiences. Mo was preparing to join him at the end of the academic year. She was passionate about the prospect.

Only Serge seemed out of place in this tableau of bliss. He was French. It was he who gave me a ride to Ed and Mary's when the soiree abruptly came to an end. Although I didn't understand why, I noticed around eight o'clock that the house was emptying out. Jean-Patrick was just then talking to me about his first Jerusalem artichoke, which he'd produced the previous year after several fruitless attempts. I listened to him politely, and as I looked around, I saw the other guests leaving very quickly, still smiling, kissing the host and hostess, a radiant couple named Emma, a naturopath, and Will, an architect.

Practically in the middle of a sentence, Jean-Patrick looked at his watch and said, "Oh, for . . ." He shook my hand and made me promise to come and see him out on his lands. The guests were vanishing like thrushes taking flight after a volley of buckshot is fired into a thicket. I found myself alone with my empty glass, which I filled again by finishing a bottle I spotted on a low table.

"Nice party?" Emma called out merrily. She was in her immense kitchen—four ovens, two refrigerators, two freezers, two toasters, two coffee makers, two electric citrus juicers, six-burner range, a variety of food processors—tossing out expensive leftovers while Will filled one of the two dishwashers.

"Great! The evening starts very well," I said.

"Yes, indeed! It was nice," she replied.

I understood—without really understanding very well, to tell the truth—that I should leave. Outside, a guy was lighting a cigarette. Gray, close-cropped hair, puffy red face, double chin, horsey teeth, belly pressing against a beige short-sleeved shirt and hanging over his belt, a briefcase clamped under one arm. In his sixties. He held out a hand to me.

"Serge."

"Philippe."

"Don't be surprised," he said, speaking in French. "It's always like that here."

"What's like what?"

"You think it's just beginning, but it's already over. Basically, what they disapprove of is pleasure. They're a people for whom pleasure is a sin. God's always there, lurking somewhere with a rod, ready to whack them one on the balls or the knuckles. Even for the less-than-true believers. Even for those who don't believe anymore."

He took a long, voluptuous drag on his cigarette. He looked a little like Dominique Strauss-Kahn, but taller and grayer.

"As you've noticed, Americans are always smiling, everywhere, at everything, at everybody, all the time. But behind the smile, there's no sincerity. No joy. No emotion. Nothing. The smile is social veneer. It's the facade. The convention. They hide everything behind it. Truth. Sorrow. Questions. Revolts. Resentments. Problems. Hatreds.

"It's the same with the ketchup they put on their grub. Everything's hiding behind it: tastes, flavors, subtleties, bitterness. Nothing gets through anymore. It all disappears behind the sugar and the agreeable but totally false sensation. Ketchup is the smile on their food. And if you think about it, it's not for nothing that mass murder is a specialty of the country. At some point, a guy gets tired of conforming to the smiling code, or the ketchup code, or the code of the party that ends before it even starts, like the one we've just been subjected to. He gets out his automatic rifle and fires into the crowd. There, at least, he enjoys himself. He throws his party. He has as good a time as he can, right to the end. Fortunately, such guys remain on the fringes. Most people prefer to suppress everything, gnaw at themselves in silence, and cultivate their nice ulcer or their pretty little cancer. Or blow their brains out."

Serge offered to drive me home. It was just a stone's throw away, but he insisted we take his car. "I can't walk very well," he said. "A problem in the lumbar region."

"Sports injury?"

"No. Too much fucking. I spent my life fucking. I can even say that nothing else interested me. And so today, I'm paying the price. You see that? Without wanting to, I'm talking like them, just from living here so long. Anyway, that's all over, all that. I don't fuck anymore. When I try to hit on someone, I always get shot down. I don't understand why, frankly. I'm still fit for human consumption. And then the Harvey Weinstein affair ruined everything. Before, you could still reel in a student or two, discreetly, of course. But now, you compliment a girl on her hair, and you're lucky if you don't get accused of sexual harassment. I think some Philip Roth novels couldn't be published today. That's what we've come to. Strange times."

It took Serge an hour to go a quarter of a mile. He needed to talk. In his native language. About himself. About his perfectly wasted life, as he liked to call it. He drove very slowly through sleeping Indiana, taking the curves while letting his thick fingers slide over the leather-covered steering wheel, as if he were caressing the curves of a hip; from time to time, he ran his tongue over his big teeth.

I'd always had a gift for collecting despairs. His was damp and solitary. What remained of all his conquests was a song of ruin, two divorces, three grown children whose first names cost him an effort to remember and who were scattered over three continents, a career nearing its end as head of the human sciences laboratory at the university, and a raging backache. "And besides," he confided to me by way of a farewell as I was getting out of his car in front of Ed and Mary's house, "I've been having a lot of trouble getting hard recently."

To which I could come up with no response.

Oddly enough, in our conversation—which could more accurately be called a monologue—Serge mentioned the Amish several times. The first time, he called them backward. Subsequently, he characterized them as yokels. And lastly, to express the fact that they might, in the final analysis, be right, he repeated several times, like a mantra, one of the fundamental precepts of their community: "You will not conform to this world that surrounds you."

Throughout my stay, I conformed to what was expected of me and to the world that surrounded me. I kept on talking to my students about European culture as if they hungered for knowledge of it. I smiled at my colleagues, who always smiled at me when our paths crossed in the corridors. Invited by one or another of them to their homes, I participated in other short parties—California wine, tasteless cheese cubes, guitar, fake wood fire—that invariably ended at eight o'clock. In fast-food restaurants and diners, I consumed tasteless meals that I drowned under torrents of ketchup. I left tips for waitresses who greeted me, all smiles, as if I'd been their best friend for twenty years. I was never invited to dinner anywhere by anybody, except once by Serge, but we didn't eat any solid food, contenting ourselves with emptying four bottles of pinot noir and one of bourbon, and with smoking a large quantity of cigarettes.

The next day was a Sunday. I got up late, with a hangover the likes of which I hadn't suffered for a long time. As usual, Mary had laid out a size XXL breakfast on the dining room table.

Next to my coffee cup, an envelope awaited me. I was opening it when Ed, with his old cowboy's gait, entered the room. He greeted me, saw the envelope, and said that one of my colleagues had dropped it off for me a little while ago.

> *Remembered that I have to leave for a lab directors' convention in San Francisco. After that, directly to Mexico, two weeks to update a university exchange system that jackass Trump wants to put in the garbage can. In 'Frisco or among the Hispanics, maybe I'll finally be able to get myself some! Never give up as long as you're not dead! Delighted to have met you. Have a good weekend.*
>
> *Serge*
>
> *P.S. Give some thought to what I told you about the Amish!*

Ed came and sat down across from me with a cup of coffee in his hand. He looked out the window and told me that it was going to be a marvelous day, that he loved the fall and its light, that it reminded him of conversations with cinematographers and gaffers on movie sets. Guys who were obsessed with light. Who thought only about light. Who talked only about light. And specifically about the famous "magic hour," which makes volumes, landscapes, objects, and living beings sublime, which caresses them, sculpts them, magnifies them.

Ed went on, saying that for some among us, the lucky ones, there was something better than the magic hour; there was the magic life, composed of a sequence of moments, each more stunning than the last. And he was one of the elect, thanks to Mary, with whom he'd lived such a life for more than fifty years.

The giant stopped talking. He took a long sip of coffee, looked me straight in the eyes, smiled a calm, sad smile, and said in his Texas accent, "But now Mary's going to die, and I'll be alone forever."

A few hours later, I was breathing the air of the countryside. Earth. Cut grass. Pig slurry. I'd left the town and driven for a while, slowly, no more than thirty miles an hour, thrusting my face out the lowered window to chase away drunkenness and melancholy, avoiding raccoon carcasses, to which I hardly paid attention anymore because there were so many of them, along with the more massive, contorted, distressing remains of deer, which seemed to have fallen off of trailers. Following Ed's directions, I stopped on a curve at the end of a forest. I was admiring the extensive, terraced view.

The sun was playing hide-and-seek behind a curtain of ash trees on top of a hill. Below it, on the left, there was a little pond amid a bed of supple reeds. A few ducks were tracing ephemeral lines on the surface of the water. A sunken lane bordered the pond on the right and led to a farm with two barns. Behind it, around it, everywhere, plowed and fallow fields.

I opened the car door and calmly got out. It's crazy how America gives impetus and grace to simple gestures and commonplace individuals: all of a sudden, I was no longer an ordinary guy stepping out of a car and walking along a path, but a character in a movie, the leading man, obviously, moving with assurance toward a fate he couldn't yet imagine.

Free-range chickens. A cat, running away. A dog on a leash, lifting one eyelid, then closing it. A shitty courtyard, cluttered with various kinds of waste. Some children, seven or eight—I couldn't manage to count them—snotty-nosed, barefoot, dirty beyond description, dressed in patched rags, using sticks to push a kind of ball made of pieces of cloth while two pigs lay in the nearby mud and watched them.

I noticed that the children were playing but not laughing. Their faces were serious, pale, taut with concentration, marked by a fixed sadness. They'd been given crude haircuts. Everything about them was dirty. The pink of their cheeks disappeared under thick crusts of dirt.

They paid no attention to me, even when I said hello, even when I raised my voice to ask if anyone was home. Only the geese replied, honking at me and running around me in a circle, the gander hissing louder than his harem, ready to charge.

Then a young woman came out. Wearing the inevitable uniform of days gone by. White bonnet, long, washed-out blue dress, gray smock. She was wiping her hands on a colorless towel. She too was barefoot. Her feet sank into the mud of the courtyard. She was almost pretty, but when you looked at her face closely, it seemed to warp along a diagonal line that shifted it to the left, tilting it as though buffeted by the force of a powerful wind. Her skin was of a medicinal whiteness. When she saw me, she opened her mouth wide, but no sound came out. She waited. The children had suddenly regrouped around her, the youngest ones groping for her hands or clasping the skirts of her dress.

I mentioned Ed's and Mary's names. I explained that they'd asked me to come and buy some eggs, and that they'd said she had some very good ones. Could she possibly sell me a dozen?

She gave me a slight nod, and after shooing away the children, who resumed their game, she went back to the door. When she reached the threshold, she turned around and indicated that I should come in.

The kitchen was big and dark. I needed some time to adjust before my eyes could distinguish details, furniture, and shapes. Two narrow windows in opposite walls let in two beams of oblique light, which met and passed each other above a big, rectangular wooden table with eleven chairs placed around it. The floor was packed earth. The furniture seemed to have traveled across time. A waterstone in a corner. Right beside it, some tin pails and jugs. A wood stove. A kind of cage with sides made of fine-mesh screen: a food safe, apparently, but I couldn't make out what foods the shapes inside corresponded to. Four candles—the only source of light after nightfall—were stuck onto a fixture suspended from the relatively low ceiling.

The young woman left me alone a moment and disappeared through a little door, which must have opened onto the henhouse. A warm smell of droppings and feathers wafted over to me, along with the sound of rustling wings, indignant cackling, and other high-pitched poultry cries.

She came back, hands joined, carrying eggs. They were still dirty, with traces of excrement that some bits of straw were clinging to. She delicately placed the eggs in an old paper bag and held it out to me. I gave her a five-dollar bill. She made a sign with her chin; the price was right. I thanked her, bid her goodbye, and left. I hadn't at any moment heard the sound of her voice.

The children outside looked even filthier than they had a few minutes earlier. The youngest was sitting down in the mud, playing with it and spreading it over his face. The others, armed with their sticks, were still running after their poor ball.

When I got back to my car and turned to gaze at the farm one last time, I noticed a column of smoke rising above the pond and into the blue air, which was trimmed with pink toward the west. It looked like there might be a fire, but it was only dust, mounting up from the earth that a man was ripping open with an ancient hand plow pulled by a horse. The man was, no doubt, the egg lady's husband. I could see only his silhouette, bent over his plow with a violence that evoked the immense, solitary, and almost desperate effort required by his work. The impression he made on me was that of an ancient hero, a cousin of Sisyphus or Prometheus, condemned to an eternal labor whose end wasn't in any way perceptible, so vast and unbridgeable was the gap between the task's terrifying magnitude and the man's smallness.

The geography of the Amish sometimes jibed with that of ordinary people. In Indiana, you might come across horse-drawn carts that were overtaking big, chromed pick-up trucks with tinted windows. Nor was it rare to see, in the aisles of the supermarkets, young students, girls dressed in shorts so tight they made their pink thighs bulge and gave them wedgies, and T-shirts that clung to their breasts and exposed navels pierced with silver nails, their arms loaded with processed food, their flip-flops revealing their painted toenails, and next to these shoppers, an Amish couple, like extras escaped from a historical film, attentively examining the products offered for sale but apparently not purchasing anything.

The only person surprised by this was me. The people here were used to these mingled presences, which rubbed against one another without speaking, which existed without concern for the members of the other group, and whose mere appearance bore witness to diametrically opposed existential choices. Nevertheless, I couldn't stop myself from thinking that it was a little like putting a contemporary individual and his or her great-great-grandfather in the same place at the same moment, each of them with their own look, their own thoughts, and their own dreams.

But if the Amish frequented the shops in the town center, the reverse occurred less often. The general population of Indiana seldom entered any of the few shops

run by members of the Amish community, as I'd figured
out myself.

In the middle of huge, hummocky fields, right under
the sky, which in that place seemed higher, loftier, stood
two clapboard sheds and an inoperable gasoline pump,
whose flaking, peacock-blue paint went together harmoni-
ously with the atolls of rust that colonized it. A warm wind
was blowing, disheveling the tall, dry grasses near a pile of
stones that might have once been a well, now filled in. Some
crows perched on a gutter were gazing into the distance. I
couldn't help thinking about the universe depicted in certain works by Grant Wood or Walker Evans, who both succeeded in capturing the soul of a rural, desolate America.

Through the wide-open door of the shed on the left,
some old hay bales were visible amid piles of indefinable
debris. Three steps led up to the entrance door of the shed
on the right. When I pushed the door open, I activated a
harsh-sounding little bell.

It would have been quite difficult to discern any unify-
ing principle in what was for sale there, because it included
a bit of everything: plates, cutlery, saucepans, frying pans,
cooking pots, cups, bowls, saws, screwdrivers, wood-carving
knives, sewing kits, milk cans, hammers, nails, screws, tri-
angles, plumb lines, string and rope of various diameters,
candlesticks, gardening dibbles, tin basins, watering cans,
braided wicker cradles, baskets, and so forth.

But what characterized all these objects was that none
of them was new. They all bore witness to repeated use and
to remarkable length of service. They weren't secondhand,
but maybe third-, fourth-, or even fifth-hand, as evidenced
by the numerous patches visible on the earthenware plates
or by the dents and cracks in the enamel of some coffee
pots.

The most striking item for sale was a veteran sewing machine, a hand crank model bearing the New Home
brand, whose painted flowers and gilding still gave off some

flashes of radiance here and there. A half-obliterated date
allowed me to ascertain the year of the machine's manu-
facture: 1896.

I had the impression of being not so much in a store
as in a kind of ethnological museum, whose single room
displayed the collected remnants of a lost civilization, and
yet the place was clearly a commercial establishment, as
indicated by the prices written by hand on pieces of slate,
as well as by the presence of a shelf where various comesti-
bles were lined up: about thirty jars, unequal in height, in
which improbable shapes floated in liquids that were, for
the most part, greenish.

It had been explained to me that the Amish habit-
ually boiled their food, whether vegetables or meat. As I
gazed at the jars on that shelf, what came to mind wasn't
the prepared meals aisle of a French delicatessen, but
the laboratory of a mad scientist, where embryos born
of crossbreedings contrary to nature were preserved in
formaldehyde.

That same day, on my way back, I passed not far from
the fields where Jean-Patrick, the ex-professor turned truck
farmer, was laboring away. When he saw me, his face lit up
as if I were the Messiah. He abandoned his hoe and had
me take what he called "the grand tour of my property,"
but he immediately corrected himself, because he didn't
have the resources to purchase those lands and was only
renting them from their actual owners.

While he was again serving me a little glass of his
abominable pear brandy—"home-distilled!"—whose
strange taste combined rubber and herring, Jean-Patrick
explained that Pennsylvania, one of the original thirteen
colonies, was established on the principles of a peaceful
relationship with the native tribes and of religious toler-
ance. This was the reason why, from the end of the seventeenth century on, Pennsylvania had welcomed several

different Anabaptist communities that had become unwelcome in many of the realms of Europe.

Among those communities were the Amish, whose beginnings brought me back to the region where I was born and still live, because it was on the Alsatian side of the Vosges mountains in northeastern France, at Sainte-Marie-aux-Mines in the val de Lièpvre, that Jakob Amman, originally from Switzerland, founded the movement in 1693, after having been welcomed onto lands belonging to the Seigneur de Ribeaupierre, a tolerant spirit who knew that those men, followers of a rigorous religious practice, were also excellent farmers.

"Another little glass of pear?"

"No, thanks. It's good, but I have to drive."

However, in 1712, toward the end of his reign, Louis XIV ordered that all Anabaptists were to be driven out of the Kingdom of France. Some of them found refuge in the Duchy of Lorraine, in the principality of Salm, in Montbéliard, before moving on to the Low Countries and then to North America, especially to lands in what would later become the state of Pennsylvania. To this day, even though English is their official language, at home the Amish still speak a Germanic tongue closely related to the Alsatian dialect.

The Amish refuse all modern civilization's contributions to daily life. They have no electricity, no motors or engines, or if they do possess one, they consider themselves forbidden to start it and ask someone else to do so. They have no system of social insurance, but they help one another. Most of them refuse to be vaccinated. The federal government has granted them the right to school their children themselves, and to stop their schooling at the age of fourteen. They've also obtained an exemption from conscription. They don't vote, and they don't interest themselves in the world's affairs. Each community holds certain assemblies at which important decisions are made. At the age of sixteen, every young man and woman is given the right, for a year, to stop obeying the rules of Amish life and to explore the universe far from their own, to go where they please, to smoke, dance, listen to music, mingle with other young people, drink.

But at the end of that year, most of them return to the community. They're too unsuited to modern life. They can't bear it.

Jean-Patrick fell silent. His plaid shirt was soaked with sweat. His thin, sunburned face looked like a martyr's, carved by an artist out of a thin piece of wood. He started talking again, in a dreamy tone, as if to himself.

"They fascinated me when I got here. Sure, there's the folklorish side, the outfits, the buggies, but that wasn't what interested me. As I observed them, I realized that they lived as though according to a kind of avatar of the very principle of a monastic community, but in theirs, men and women would be mixed together. Their space is open, but they've recreated the monastery or abbey walls, virtual walls that separate them from the world and the age, as someone said. They incarnate a regular, open form of existence. They're in an elastic bubble that simultaneously defies both our space and our time. It's tremendous, when you think about it: they're here and now, but that here and that now have nothing to do with ours."

On the eve of my departure, I took my last spin. The forests were turning reddish-brown. The green was retreating, as if swallowed up by the fire devouring the foliage. I seemed to see fewer raccoon carcasses on the sides of the roads. Big storms were gathering in the sky, and the air smelled like ice pellets and dry meadows.

On rising ground between two horse pastures, an Amish man was walking along the side of the road. Slowly. Limping, I thought, on his left leg. I drew even with him, stopped, lowered my window, and greeted him. He was a very old man with a beard that reached the middle of his chest. His spectacles had circular iron rims. His lively eyes pierced the shadow that his big hat cast over half of his face. I asked if he would like a ride. He accepted with a chin movement, but he remained standing where he was, beside the door. I realized that I was supposed to get out and open it for him. Which I did. He settled in, not removing his black felt hat, which got squashed against the Impala's ceiling. I started driving again.

He had yet to speak a word. I tried to begin a conversation, but he responded to everything I said with a kind of murmur, not completely friendly, but not completely unpleasant either. All at once, it occurred to me to speak to him in German, and I dug around in my memory of the distant past for recollections of my studies in that language. I asked him where he was going. He looked at me with sudden interest and answered me with words whose meaning I guessed rather than understood; they sounded mispronounced, lopsided, in comparison with a standard way of speaking German.

And so it was that the two of us—I in my bad student's mishmash and he in his uprooted dialect transmitted from generation to generation, deformed by the years and the forgetting, the mistakes and the gaps—attempted, during our short drive, to talk about fields, the land, and God.

When we arrived at his farm, which was hidden behind an immense willow plantation, he waited for me to get out of the car and open his door for him. Four young men, beardless and therefore unmarried—for every Amish man starts growing his beard on his wedding day, and not before—came out to meet us.

They seemed relieved to recover the old man and surrounded him, speaking in low voices. With their violent haircuts, where the traces of the scissors-massacre could still be seen, and their spacious trousers, which exposed their ankles and which their suspenders pulled up above their waists, with their torn and crudely mended shirts and their feral, very pale faces, they might have been taken for musicians in an alternative rock band getting ready to pose for Annie Leibovitz.

The old man was speaking to them and gesturing toward me from time to time. They all looked at me benevolently. I was waiting by the car. He came back to me and asked where I lived. In any case, that's what I thought he said. Rather than launch into impossible explanations, I squatted down to the ground, picked up a stick lying nearby, and started drawing in the dust, and in broad outline, the North American continent, France, and Europe. Then I thrust the stick into a spot in the dust that represented, more or less, Pennsylvania.

"*Hier!*" I said, waving a finger at the farm and everything surrounding it.

The four youths and the old fellow repeated the word, nodding their heads.

Next I pointed the stick at the Atlantic, made them understand that it was the ocean, a great big sea. "*See, grosser See,*" I said, and finally placed the stick on the eastern half of France. "*Mein Haus,*" I said, patting the region of my heart with the palm of my hand. "*Mein Haus.* Sainte-Marie-aux-Mines. Jakob Amman."

The four youngsters turned toward the old man, who was looking at me with great surprise in his eyes. They pressed him with questions. He commenced a monologue of which I understood not a word, but I let myself be lulled by the music, simultaneously mineral and cheerful, of the exhumed dialect, which wrapped around me like a magical linen cloth, suddenly removing me from the place where I was and transporting me to a neither utterly unknown nor utterly familiar elsewhere.

When he was finished talking, the old man made a sign to the young ones, who bade me farewell and withdrew.

He stood facing me and grasped both my hands. Because I was taller than he was, he raised his head a little, and when he did the light fell on his forehead, where numerous wrinkles drew parallel furrows. He had very bright gray eyes, and his eyeglasses gave him the look of a wise old man.

"Jakob Amman. *Ei richig Mann! Ei heilig Mann! E wa lange herr!*"

He shook my hands, squeezing them, and repeated his words, sounding almost melancholy: "*E wa lange herr . . .*"

Then he released his grip, let my hands go, saluted me with a motion of his head, and turned his back. I waited until he reentered his farmhouse before I got back in my Chevrolet. I started the engine and drove off slowly, accompanied by the singing of the crickets, by the first streaks of lightning, which was eviscerating the heavy clouds, and by the rumble of thunder in the distance.

I rolled down my window and stuck out my head.

The sudden air began to grow fragrant with the smell of rain and fresh grass.

Just like home.

LAS VEGAS

By
Alice Zeniter

Translated by
Emma Ramadan

f, when you think about Las Vegas, you imagine a skyline similar to New York's, which is to say perforated by skyscrapers, you should forget it, or at least challenge it. The only horizon line you'll find in Vegas is on the Strip, the famous row of hotel-casinos, and it exists—like everything on that part of South Las Vegas Boulevard—only to imitate cities that are not Vegas, those that Vegas duplicates and appropriates as it pleases. The Vegas skyline—outlined by the wing at the top of the Bellagio, the golden rectangle of Trump Tower, the twin curves of the Wynn hotels, or even the supposedly medieval turrets of the Excalibur—is as typically Vegas as the reconstruction of St. Mark's Square in the Las Vegas Palazzo or the loose replica of the Tuileries in the Paris Las Vegas.

There are two schools of thought about this: one side claims that the real Vegas is precisely that ludicrous imitation, so omnipresent on the Strip that it ends up eclipsing its models (the truth of Vegas is in fact illusion), and the other side insists the real Vegas is the 99 percent of the city that is not the Strip, the one the majority of tourists have no idea exists. It's not that I'd already chosen a camp upon arrival, but I said to myself that I'd already seen the Strip in movies, and decided I'd rather rent a room between the Arts District and Huntridge.

If there's a local architecture, it is decidedly low: one-story houses, stores twenty times as wide as they are tall, platbands of red stones planted with a few pudgy cacti.

Above the buildings is an immense sky and, all around the city, mountains. I'm told you can see the tiny white cap of eternal snow on some, but I can't make it out. However, I marvel at the sky. I don't think I've ever seen so much of it.

The Street

Defying the flat architecture, palm trees reach toward the endless azure. A forest of billboards, advertisements solidly planted on their two metal legs, accompany the trees as they climb. Here, they mostly promote the services of lawyers flaunting huge smiles and various specialties ("ARRESTED? INJURED? CALL ED!"). On Charleston Boulevard, a sign asks: "ACCIDENT? IMMIGRATION? BANKRUPTCY?" positing the three as equally random catastrophes in human life.

One morning, I witness a car accident on one of the six terrifying roads that run through my neighborhood, and the two drivers involved get out of their cars, telephones glued to their ears. I imagine they're already calling their lawyers because they both have that exaggerated, serious look on their faces like they're speaking to someone official—which doesn't stop one of them from covering her cell phone's microphone from time to time to scream at the other: "YOU'RE A DUMB CUNT!" I watch the scene from the sidewalk, pummeled by the sun of Bonneville Avenue, since this was during the time I was still trying to walk in Vegas. I'd give up on that the next day.

With the exception of tourists on the Strip and on Fremont—the main street in "old Vegas"—no one walks. The sidewalks are nearly deserted; there are only the homeless people, sitting in the rare corners of shade, under the lowest trees. Hidden by the foliage and their pocket of darkness, I notice them only as I'm about to pass, the rustling of a plastic bag, nails scratching a scalp. In those neighborhoods with low and spaced-out houses, shade is a rare commodity along the ultra-wide thoroughfares and, when it's 113 degrees Fahrenheit, absolutely necessary. When I step outside, the heat seems less like a meteorological figure and more like the blast resulting from a massive explosion or the aftermath of a fire in a distant forest. It burns my eyelids, my eyes, my throat. After twenty minutes in the street, every square inch of exposed skin becomes painful.

On the second day, I get lost trying to reach Fremont from Paseos Park. My heart rate speeds up, white discs appear in front of my eyes. The drivers stare at me with surprise and sometimes disgust (I'd already noticed the strange reactions pedestrians provoke in the United States when I visited Mississippi and Tennessee with my sisters a few years earlier). Walking in this desert city requires a comprehensive strategy, one I try to implement for a few days. At crosswalks, I seek out the thin line of shade from the streetlights to protect me as much as possible from the sun. Each time I identify a building tall enough to project a shadow that can accommodate me entirely, I stop for several minutes. During one of these pauses I notice there isn't a single public bench in this part of Vegas. On the Strip, there are. But on the Strip, there are no homeless people, or very few, because the police drive them out regularly. No benches, no water fountains in the street—only in the parks. The only weapon against the heat is the smattering of trees, and under each of them, I find a body sitting, crouched down, or sprawled.

Depending on the year, Las Vegas ranks third or fourth among American cities most affected by homelessness (in proportion to the total population). There are very few homeless shelters and, according to several humanitarian associations, the local authorities have primarily aesthetic concerns: the actions taken consist mainly in displacing the homeless to keep them from insinuating themselves into the visible areas of the city. Later in the week, Sara (I'll come back to her) points at a 7-Eleven in the north of the city, saying: "Here, they blast classical music in the parking lot to make them leave." I imagine that any music played at full volume would chase away anyone who hoped to settle in front of the convenience store, but in their choice of classical music, I perceive a profound contempt of class: "A sonata? It's perfect! Those poor people won't understand it at all. They'll take off running!"

Reading *Dream*, by Stephen Duncombe, I realize to what extent Las Vegas is a rich city that ignores or despises its poor: "Nevada has the second highest potential tax revenue of all the states, yet the taxes it collects are the third lowest in the country . . . When it comes to public education, the state spends $1,100 less per student than Mississippi. Nevada is thirty-eighth in the nation in health services, and it is fifty-first in Medicaid spending (after Washington, D.C.)." Online, I learn that there are numerous reasons for the alarming number of homeless people and why they sadly seem to pile up here. The first is Vegas's geographic position: surrounded by mountains and the uninhabitable desert, the city's poverty is concentrated in a limited area. The second is that the main psychiatric hospital in Nevada lacks the resources to accommodate its patients for a long period of time and regularly releases them into the wild with a week's supply of medication. Finally, Las Vegas is Las Vegas, which is nothing but a lazy statement of the obvious.

In addition to the local poverty, you have to take into account that men and women whose lives have just crumbled or are teetering like a Jenga tower cross the country to come here in the hope of "starting over." They refuse to accept that at the end of the day, "the house always wins," except maybe in the movies. You have to question the role Hollywood has played in nurturing the obsessive hope that many Americans, fueled by iconic gambling movies, place in casinos and their godlike ability to suddenly abolish poverty. When these men and women wind up penniless,

they are far from the safety net created by human relationships and support systems. They don't have any family or
friends in the city, and that's when their brutal experience
on the street begins.

I put an end to my own time on the street after a few
days and decided to use Lyft. Beyond the physical unpleas-
antness brought on by the blazing sun ("a scorching heat,"
as they say in Vegas), I'm not comfortable in the street. Why
would a woman with money insist on sharing the sidewalk
with the most impoverished? To witness that they're there?
But I don't even speak to them! I am a woman alone in a
public space, a situation I perceive as potentially dangerous,
and I speed up automatically, stare at the sidewalk, and
don't respond when they call to me. In these conditions,
I'm better off sticking with cars, even if it means I'll forget,
to an extent, the silhouettes sheltered under the trees.

No One Is from Las Vegas

A few days after my arrival, I meet Sara Ortiz. Sara is from
Austin, Texas. She moved here in the spring of 2018 to
be the program manager of the Black Mountain Institute
(BMI) and of the literary journal *The Believer*, which was
established in California before migrating to Las Vegas two
years ago. In the BMI offices, I find a collection of Toni
Morrison's poetry, published in 2002 in a print run of a few
hundred copies. A few days after her death, I am moved to
find myself looking at "Five Poems" that I didn't know she
had written. Sara opens the book carefully ("Shit," she says,
recalling her former archivist days, "I should have put on
gloves."), and we read: "I would do it all over again: / Be
the harbor and set the sail, / Loose the breeze and har-
ness the gale, / Cherish the harvest of what I have been.
/ Better the summit to scale. / Better the summit to be."

The BMI offices are directly opposite the Marjorie
Barrick Museum, where I've just been to an exhibition

by Justin Favela and Ramiro Gomez titled "Sorry for the Mess." A study of the immigrant workers who maintain the hotel-casinos, the exhibition presents portraits of men and women in uniform, on big cardboard panels. There are also immense yellow signs warning "Caution Wet Floor" and crepe-paper reproductions of the game table felts and the carpets of the most famous casinos on the Strip. Sara is the daughter of Salvadoran immigrants; her mother was a hospital cleaner. She tells me she couldn't stop crying at the gallery opening. Some of the subjects depicted by Gomez were stepping into a museum for the first time when they came to see the show, timid, intimidated, and proud. Alisha Kerlin, the museum director, tells me that the show will now be installed in Las Cruces, New Mexico. It's the first time an exhibition of local artists, curated for a museum in Vegas, will travel across the country. "It will boost the confidence of all the artists in the city's contemporary art scene," she says, and Sara vigorously agrees—she is often riled up by the disdainful grins that appear on people's faces in American cultural capitals when they talk about Vegas, "even though they know nothing about it."

During my trip, I was frequently told that life is good here. "We stay for the sunset over the desert, and because we can drink a glass of wine on a patio with friends all year round," a splendid redheaded woman tells me at the Velveteen Rabbit bar. She came here to dance in one of the shows on the Strip. After ten years, she took a job in communications for the Performing Arts Center at the University of Nevada. "I'm here because there's always work," Mickäel, one of my Lyft drivers, tells me. "Because there's good technical training and I didn't want to be in the military anymore," says Anthony, who just moved to town after six years in the army. "It's less expensive than LA," says Rebecca. "Because I couldn't stay in Chicago," says MJ, "the streets are too rough over there and I knew I would have ended up in some bullshit." "Because this is the only place where you can meet so many different people, almost all of them crazy, and then go back home where it's nice and quiet." No one is from Vegas, but there seem to be a million reasons to live in Vegas.

A bartender at Atomic Liquors admitted to me that he came here because he's a golfer: "And since it's over a hundred degrees here three months of the year, there aren't many people who can stand to be on the course. So the annual memberships are cheap." It might seem absurd, but Vegas attracts people for far stranger reasons. In the 1950s, the city was a hotbed of "nuclear tourism." The Nevada chamber of commerce published a calendar of nuclear tests done in the desert—119 explosions between 1951 and 1958—and entire families rushed here to picnic and admire the show. Buses stopped outside the Strip hotels to bring tourists to the sites, and souvenir shops slapped mushroom clouds on every possible surface. That's where Atomic Liquors, one of the oldest bars in Vegas, gets its name: customers used to gather on the roof to watch the explosions. In 1963, the tests went underground, and people had to find other ways to draw visitors to Vegas.

The city and the hotel industry are constantly trying to increase the mass of tourists. A visit to the Neon Museum provides a quick overview. It's an ossuary of defunct signs, some still flickering, surrounded by the familiar buzzing of neon, and the collection outlines the entire history of Vegas. Steve, Sara's partner, is a museum guide from Illinois. In front of a giant skull on the desert soil, he tells me that at the beginning of the 1990s, jealous of Disneyland's success, promoters thought Vegas might be missing out on enormous amounts of money by not "tapping into" the families scared off by the nickname "Sin City." So they decided to develop a family-friendly side, opening amusement parks as well as the enormous hotel-casino Treasure Island. This "pirates' paradise" puts on a spectacle of sirens and adopts the enormous skull behind Steve as its logo.

Alas, the project is a failure. Families don't want to come to Vegas. The skull is taken down, the sirens are sacked, replaced with a shopping center, and the city, in an attempt to rekindle its sinful reputation, launches a publicity campaign based on the now famous slogan "What Happens in Vegas Stays in Vegas."

At the end of the visit, Steve, Sara, and I head to Frankie's Tiki Room on Charleston. From the outside, it doesn't look like much, located right off of an enormous intersection. Not far away is a tire store open twenty-four hours a day that sometimes organizes DJ sets outside its gigantic garage door that absolutely no one attends—even the store employees hide behind the towers of tires. It's dark inside Frankie's, and between bamboo partitions, groups smoke and play cards. The tables are sticky with rum, and all the cocktails are sickly sweet. One of Las Vegas's nicknames (the third I've named now) is "Hawaii's ninth island." Fifty thousand Hawaiians live here, and one out of every ten Hawaiians comes to Vegas every year. The close relationship between the archipelago and the city is thanks to a casino boss named Sam Boyd, who lived in Hawaii for some time and noticed the islanders' passion for gambling. In the 1950s, Boyd started to build an empire in Vegas. Twenty years later, when his businesses were struggling, Boyd had the idea to bring Hawaiians over. He deployed an arsenal of seduction based on "vacation packages" that included low-cost flights, hotels at heavily discounted rates, and traditional island dishes. Even today, four flights chartered by Boyd Gaming make the trip between Hawaii and Vegas each week.

Strippers and Unions

In the Arts District, in addition to galleries, antique shops, and hip cafés, there's also the Burlesque Hall of Fame. The pink walls display photos of naked women alongside several strings of glass beads. A chronological frieze depicts a time-line of the evolution of the striptease and the lap dance. When I enter, an old man is being firmly escorted to the door because "he tried to come take a look for free again."

However, this is not a place of seedy voyeurism. The young guide who welcomes me is wearing a T-shirt printed with the words "Pussy Power." Her heroines are Jennie Lee ("the Bazoom Girl" or "the burlesque version of Jayne Mansfield") and Gypsy Rose Lee ("the intellectual stripper"). Gypsy, who was a star in the 1930s, was famous for reciting poetry to her audience as she stripped. A big Proust fan, she wrote two detective novels and a memoir and asked the journalist H. L. Mencken ("the Sage of Baltimore" or "the American Nietzsche") to find a more dignified term than stripper to describe her profession. And so Gypsy Rose Lee was the first ecdysiast. As for Jennie Lee, her Wikipedia page describes her as a "stripper and union activist"—I don't think there could be a more marvelously concise biography. Lee started the first union of exotic dancers in Los Angeles and fought relentlessly for higher salaries. She was the one who patiently assembled the majority of the pieces in that little museum, which was originally located on her California ranch and only recently moved to Las Vegas.

Lee's ranch also housed retired dancers, because Jennie Lee knew to what extent a career as a stripper could weigh on romantic relationships: most of the time, the "girls" remained alone, remained girls, and there was no one to take care of them in their old age. There are several photographs of those aging women, sometimes frankly, joyously old, breasts exposed, flesh overflowing their sparkly costumes, their bodies the opposite of what I'd seen on Fremont or on the Strip, in underwear or sequins or leather.

Las Vegas is the stripping capital, and on the touristy streets there are dozens of men and women with scrupulously stereotypical bodies promoting a hostess bar, a Chippendales show, or a topless cabaret, brochures in their hands and butts exposed. Staring at those bodies that all look alike, it would be impossible to guess what I learn from the guide at the Burlesque Hall of Fame, which is that Carrie Finnell, the first to add tassels and jewelry to pasties, weighed two hundred pounds at the height of her stripping career, and she packed the house for fifty-four consecutive weeks when she launched the longest striptease in the world in the 1920s.

Not long after I discovered the existence of Jennie Lee's Exotic Dancers' League, I heard about another union, more current and much more powerful: the Culinary Workers Union. I admit that when I landed in Vegas, I hadn't expected to hear so much praise for trade unions. But as we drink beers at Atomic Liquors, a patron named Steve, sitting next to me at the bar, asks me if I plan to write about the Culinary Union.

The union is made up of sixty thousand restaurant industry workers in Las Vegas and Reno. Their website reads: "Solidarity resources: know your rights, protect yourself, your family, and your coworkers." The restaurant industry in Nevada employs men and women from 160 different countries, a large majority of whom are Latinx. Not all of them are documented.

The fate of immigrants in the United States is all over the news during my stay. The massacres in El Paso and Dayton happened a few days before my arrival, and Jimmy Aldaoud died at the beginning of my stay. Aldaoud, about forty years old, was deported in June 2019 from the United States to Iraq—where he'd never lived—and on Tuesday, August 6, he died because he wasn't able to obtain his diabetes medication. "Trump's policies kill," repeat the Democrats campaigning for the presidency in 2020.

If ICE agents raid your workplace, if ICE agents stop your car, if ICE agents knock on the door of your home— the Culinary Workers Union lists all possible cases and emphasizes each time: "You have the right to remain silent."

Since April 2019, the union has been in a public battle with the Palms, a hotel-casino on the Strip. At the beginning of spring, 84 percent of its nine hundred employees voted to join the Culinary Workers Union, but management refuses to acknowledge this vote or negotiate with the union. For the last several months, workers have been organizing a picket line in front of the Palms. They've received support from several Democratic candidates, including Bernie Sanders and Pete Buttigieg. It turns out that the owners of the Palms, the Fertitta brothers, are fervent Trump supporters.

"It's good to have a strong union with several thousand people," sighs Steve, who's from the Appalachian Mountains. He works as a rigger for dancers' ropes, cables, and hooks, and does not belong to a union. "Because life here can be brutal economically. Take me, for example. I have no social security. Last week, I had to get six stitches and it cost me six hundred bucks. If my car breaks down, I can't go to work, so I'd have to buy a new one right away to keep cash coming in. It haunts me: the idea that my car might break down." Liam, the waiter, a giant in his twenties, says he's not a union member. Steve chastises him. Outside, the sun sets, and the sky turns a violent pink over the mountains.

Fear and Hacking in Las Vegas

"Normally I'd put on music, but today, I turned everything off: WiFi, Bluetooth. There's a hacker conference at Bally's and you never know what those guys might do."

Walter, driving an enormous blue electric car, is right to be cautious, but I would have preferred he put on the radio: instead, I listen to him list each of his fifteen firearms, all of which he deems essential "because they don't do exactly the same thing."

I point at the round badge shining around my neck. "I know. I was at the Paris Hotel. I just left the conference."

Paris and Bally's are two hotel-casinos on the Strip, with halls full of slot machines and game tables, connected by tunnels lined with restaurants and shops. The two have gigantic convention centers that opened their doors from August 8–12 for the twenty-seventh edition of DEF CON—a conference on information security. As soon as I step into the air-conditioned depths of Paris on Thursday morning, it's exactly the hallucination I envisioned, a narcotic image the Surrealists would have envied.

Picture the Paris Las Vegas: a fake French city made from cardboard cut-outs and a painted sky, two-by-fours, streetlights, an overabundance of tassels, and an unfortunate onslaught of definite articles: Le Bar, La Cave, La Crêperie, Le Car Rental. Outside there's a small-scale version of the Arc de Triomphe and the Eiffel Tower. The decor is trying to be elegant and cutesy. Do you have the image in your head? Now, add hordes of hackers sitting all over the rugs, strewn with cables, wearing luminous hats, trampled by groups of bearded men in front of La Crêperie to have La Crêpe au Jambon (or maybe even La Crêpe à Le Jambon), dressed in T-shirts with varying degrees of menacing messages ("If it ain't broke, it will be," "My fridge could hack your smartphone"), speaking all the languages of the world and brandishing ridiculous objects, like rubber chickens and plush pineapples. (A "pineapple" is a tool used to test a WiFi connection, but I still have no idea what the rubber chicken is about.) The tourists who come to take a photo in front of the model Louvre are flabbergasted. To be honest, the DEF CON crowd is not the most handsome in the world, with their obesity, baldness, myopia, and a few provocative socks-and-sandals combos. For the couples looking for a romantic moment in Paris, the crowd probably dulls the charm of the place, spoils it, disfigures it, whereas I feel the constant desire to burst into laughter.

But the DEF CON participants shouldn't be reduced to a visual cliché, even if they lend themselves to it perfectly.

There is a pirate philosophy that surpasses the shabby spectacle of flashing LED lights, encouraging us to take back control over commercial objects by studying and modifying them, bending the technology to our desire rather than letting the aforementioned objects assign us predefined actions. As the Chaos Computer Club, a group of Berlin hackers, says, using a kettle to cook a sausage instead of to make tea is already a form of pirating. The first conference presenter to talk opens his speech with a Deleuze quote. Another lets Thoreau's *Walden* fall out of his bag as the group converses under the painted sky and starts to talk about civil disobedience. In a room reserved for "physical hacking," I learn to pick a lock thanks to volunteers from TOOOL (The Open Organization of Lockpickers), and I fail miserably at defusing a bomb. A few steps away, a dozen people attempt to take control in record time of the dashboard computer of a large Hummer decorated with shiny garlands.

"I'm not saying they're bad guys, but they hack ATMs and elevators," Walter whispers, the sight of my badge making him nervous.

Questioned about his practices, Philippe, a French man living in Portland and employed by McAfee, shrugs: those are just rumors. But soon after, he tells me I should walk around the commercial hacking village: I can learn how to hack an air conditioner.

The second night, the pool on the roof of the Paris Hotel starts to leak, and the flood forces the restaurants and shops below to close for a few hours. "Wow," posts a participant on the DEF CON Twitter account, "the guys from the 'Pirate the Pool' workshop went a little overboard this year." After such an incident, I imagine the rumors won't stop anytime soon. But after all, in the words of a character from *The Man Who Shot Liberty Valance*: "This is the West. When the fact becomes legend, print the legend."

A CALL TO YOUNG WRITERS ON THE EVE OF THE TRUMP PRESIDENCY

By
Colum McCann

Dear Young Writer,

We are in danger of having the passion of our calling robbed from us. The crisis of our age is that we are living in stunned submission to the circumstances of the times. I will not even mention his name, but, let's face it, he is not alone. We have allowed ourselves to become handcuffed by the rule of bureaucrats and hedge fund managers and politicians and others in their closed-neck shirts. We are being bought off by our affair with the contemporary drug of choice: case. At the same time, twisted social outrages are unfolding at our feet. Universities invest in fossil fuel industries. Corporations celebrate themselves as wooden boards go up on windows all around the country. Guns can be bought in our supermarkets. Mindless chatter erupts about building walls and keeping out immigrants. Books are considered so tepid that they're not even burned any-more. The problem with so much of our current reality is that it operates from a flat surface, a screen, and it does not address itself to the contoured world we live in. So, young writer, get off the couch. Get out the door. Onto the page. All of it is useless if this is just a pep talk. Your words are not a consolation prize. Have rage. Take plea-sure in the recklessness of your own imagination. So much writing nowadays seems to suffer from a reduced moral authority, not just in the minds of the readers, but in the minds and indeed the language of the writers ourselves.

Writing is no longer part of our national idea. We don't
look to our authors in the way we did decades ago. Nobody
fears what we have to say. Why is that? We have allowed
our voices to be devalued in favor of comfort. Our moral
compass is off-kilter. We have given in to the tendency
to be neutralized. We live in a culture where increasingly
we are mapped—we have GPS'd ourselves to death. We
have forgotten how to get properly lost. This is not some
bleeding-heart simplicity, nor will your response to it be.
So, embrace the challenge. Never forget that writing is the
freedom to articulate yourself against power. It is a form of
nonviolent engagement and civil disobedience. You have
to stand outside society, beyond coercion, intimidation,
cruelty, duress. Where power wants to simplify, you should
complicate. Where power wants to moralize, you should
criticize. Where power wants to intimidate, embrace. The
amazing thing about good writing is that it can find the
pulse of the wound without having to inflict the actual violence. It is a way of recognizing the hurt without praising
it or suffering it. Writing allows the illusion of pain, while
forcing us to grow up and recognize our own demons. We
touch the electricity of suffering, but we can, eventually,
recover. We carry the scars, but that's all they are: scars.
We have to understand that language is power, no matter
how often power tries to strip us of language. Want to
know your enemy? Read their books. Watch their plays.
Examine their poetry. Try to get to the heart of them. The
grievance you know is so much better than the unknown.
The impulse to know comes from encountering the multiple and complex shades of the world. Be aware of what
you are writing against. Stand up. Be aware that to be
a hero, you might have to be able to be the fool. Alas,
poor Yorick, poor Citizen, poor Falstaff, the role of the
hero often seems ridiculous, but the best of them are willing to play it anyway. Against war. Against greed. Against
walls. Against simplicity. Against shallow ignorance. The

fool should speak the truth, even when—or maybe especially when—it's unpopular. Don't be embarrassed. Don't give up. Don't be cowed into silence. Stand on the outside. Become more dangerous. Have people fear your bite. Restore that which has been devalued by others. Don't let the passion of your calling be ridiculed. Raise your voice on behalf of those who have been drowned out. Don't allow the begrudgers to render you useless. Value the cynic. Yes, praise him even. He is useful. He is one you can still teach. Don't back away from engagement. You must talk about the grime and the poverty and the injustice and the thousand other everyday torments. You must speak of life no matter how bitter or lacerating. Our writing is a living portrait of ourselves. Good sentences have the ability to shock, seduce, and drag us out of our stupor. Be what a diamond is to glass. Scrape your way across. Transform what has been seen. Imagine the immensities of experience. Oppose the cruelties. Break the silence. Be prepared to risk yourself. Find radiance. Ready yourself for scorn. Embrace difficulty. Work hard. Your song will exact a price. Be prepared to pay. Write, young writer, write. Claim your proper future. Claim your proper country. Don't let them steal it from you. Find the language to recover what we know is there. Write for the sheer pleasure we take in doing it, yes, but also for the knowledge that it can shift this beautiful, strange, furious world of ours. Literature reminds us that all life is not already written down. Change can occur. There are still infinite possibilities. Make from your confrontation with despair a tiny little margin of beauty. The more you choose to see, the more you will see. In the end, the only things worth doing are the things that might break your heart. So, break your heart, young writer. Rage on. And always be aware that the president you get doesn't have to be the country you will get.

Yours.

CONTRIBUTOR NOTES

David and Nicole Ball have translated over twenty books, together or separately, by such authors as Abdourahman Waberi, Lola Lafon, Laurent Mauvignier, Noëlle Revaz, and Michelle Lesbre, as well as multiple shorter pieces for a variety of publications, or for online magazines such as *WWB* (*Words Without Borders*). David's latest translation is Léon Werth, *Deposition 1940–1944: A Secret Diary of Life in Vichy France*, which he also edited. His *Diary of the Dark Years: 1940–1944* won the French-American Foundation's 2014 translation prize in nonfiction, and his *Darkness Moves: An Henri Michaux Anthology, 1927–1984* won MLA's prize for literary translation in 1995. He is Professor Emeritus of French and Comparative Literature at Smith College. Nicole has translated Maryse Condé into English. Her translations into French include a Jonathan Kellerman thriller and, most recently, Youssef Daoudi's graphic biography of Thelonius Monk, which won the 2018 French Jazz Academy prize. Both are members of ALTA (American Literary Translation Association). David was its president from 2003 to 2005.

Philippe Besson is an author, screenwriter, and playwright. He is the author of *Lie with Me*, a number one French bestseller and winner of the Maison de la Presse Prize, and his first novel, *In the Absence of Men*, was awarded the

Emmanuel-Roblès Prize in 2001. His other works include *His Brother* and *The Accidental Man*. His books have been translated into twenty different languages.

Julien Bisson is a French journalist now based in Paris, after having lived in Naples and San Francisco. After serving as the editor in chief of the literary magazine *Lire*, he helped to create the magazine *America*, for which he has served as the editor in chief since 2017. He is also the editor in chief for the weekly magazine *Le 1*, a television presenter for France Info, and a regular radio commentator.

François Busnel is a French journalist based in Paris. He has notably served as the managing editor for the magazine *Lire* and an editorialist for the weekly magazine *L'Express* and has hosted many radio shows for France Inter. Since 2008, he has hosted and produced the weekly literary talk show *La Grande Librairie*, broadcast in prime time on France 5. He has produced several documentaries on American writers, including Philip Roth and Jim Harrison, and he created the magazine *America* in the days after the election of Donald Trump.

Philippe Claudel is the author of many novels, including *Brodeck*, which won the Prix Goncourt des Lycéens in 2007 and the Independent Foreign Fiction Prize in 2010; *By a Slow River*; *Monsieur Linh and His Child*; and *The Investigation*. Claudel also wrote and directed the 2008 film *I've Loved You So Long*, starring Kristin Scott Thomas, which won a BAFTA Award for Best Film Not in the English Language.

Philippe Coste is a New York–based French journalist. He has been the US correspondent for *America* since its launch in 2017, writing on different topics around the country, such as the oil industry in Oklahoma, abortion in Little Rock, Arkansas, and the uninsured in the Midwest.

Philippe also freelances for European publications and is working on a book. He started covering the United States in the '90s as a staff correspondent for *L'Express* and the literary monthly *Lire*.

John Cullen was born and raised in New Orleans and received his graduate education at the Universities of Virginia and Texas. He is the translator of many books from Spanish, French, German, Italian, and Greek, including Manuel de Lope's *The Wrong Blood*, Margaret Mazzantini's *Don't Move*, Philippe Claudel's *Brodeck*, Christa Wolf's *Medea*, Patrick Modiano's *Villa Triste*, and Kamel Daoud's *The Meursault Investigation*. He lives on the shoreline in southern Connecticut.

Marie Darrieussecq, born in Bayonne, France, is a writer and psychoanalyst. In 1996, she published *Truismes*, her widely acclaimed first book, which was later translated as *Pig Tales* in English. In 2013, she was awarded the Prix Médicis and the Prix des Prix for her novel *Men: A Novel of Cinema and Desire*.

Kate Deimling has translated both fiction and nonfiction from French, including books on fashion, art history, business, and the wine industry. She holds a PhD in French literature from Columbia University and previously worked as a professor and an art journalist. She lives in Brooklyn with her family.

Joël Dicker was born in Geneva, Switzerland, and spent childhood summers in New England. He is the author of *The Truth About the Harry Quebert Affair*, winner of the Grand Prix du Roman from the Académie Française and finalist for the Prix Goncourt, as well as *The Baltimore Boys* and *The Disappearance of Stephanie Mailer*. His books have been translated into more than forty languages.

Louise Erdrich is the author of *The Round House*, which won the National Book Award for Fiction in 2012, and a two-time winner of the National Book Critics Circle Award for her novels *Love Medicine* and *LaRose*. Erdrich has received the Library of Congress Prize in American Fiction, the prestigious PEN/Saul Bellow Award for Achievement in American Fiction, and the Dayton Literary Peace Prize. She is an enrolled member of the Turtle Mountain Band of Chippewa Indians and is the owner of Birchbark Books in Minneapolis, Minnesota.

Penny Hueston's translations from French include novels by Emmanuelle Pagano (*One Day I'll Tell You Everything*), Patrick Modiano (*Little Jewel*), Sarah Cohen-Scali (*Max*), and Raphaël Jerusalmy (*Evacuation*). She has translated six books by Marie Darrieussecq—*All the Way, Men, Being Here: The Life of Paula Modersohn-Becker, Our Life in the Forest, The Baby*, and *Crossed Lines*. She has been shortlisted for the JQ-Wingate Prize, for the Scott Moncrief Prize, and twice for the New South Wales Premier's Translation Prize.

Laura Kasischke is the author of nine collections of poetry and seven novels. Her work has received many honors, including the Pushcart Prize, the Juniper Prize for Poetry, the Rilke Prize, and the National Book Critics Circle Award for Poetry. Her most recent book, *Where Now: New and Selected Poems*, was published in 2017. She teaches at the University of Michigan MFA program in Ann Arbor.

Alain Mabanckou grew up in Pointe-Noire, in the Republic of the Congo. His first novel, *Blue-White-Red*, won the Grand prix littéraire d'Afrique noire in 1999. His other books include *African Psycho, Broken Glass, Memoirs of a Porcupine*, and *Black Moses*. His work has been translated into fifteen languages, and he is a professor in the French department at the University of California, Los Angeles.

Alex Marzano-Lesnevich is the author of *The Fact of a Body: A Murder and a Memoir*, which received a Lambda Literary Award and the Prix France Inter-JDD, an award for one book of any genre in the world. Marzano-Lesnevich has written for the *New York Times*, the *New York Times Sunday Magazine*, the *Boston Globe*, and many other publications. They are an assistant professor at Bowdoin College and teach in the Pan-European low-residency MFA program.

Colum McCann was born in Dublin and lives in New York. He is the author of *Let the Great World Spin*, which won the National Book Award in 2009, as well as *TransAtlantic*, *Thirteen Ways of Looking*, and *Letters to a Young Writer*. His work has been translated into thirty-five languages and appeared in the *New Yorker*, *Esquire*, the *Paris Review*, and many others.

Jessica Moore is an award-winning poet and translator. Her first collection, *Everything, now,* is a love letter to the dead and a conversation with her translation of *Turkana Boy*, by Jean-François Beauchemin. Her translation of *Mend the Living* was nominated for the Man Booker International Prize. Moore's forthcoming poetic work is called *The Whole Singing Ocean*.

Yann Perreau is a writer, journalist, and critic. He is the author of *Londres en mouvement* and *California Dreaming*, two portraits of cities and their inhabitants. In 2017, he published a history of anonymity entitled *Incognito*. He lives in Paris and Los Angeles.

Richard Powers is the author of twelve novels. His most recent, *The Overstory*, won the Pulitzer Prize in Fiction in 2019. He is also the recipient of a MacArthur Fellowship and the National Book Award, and he has been a four-time National Book Critics Circle Award finalist. He lives in the foothills of the Great Smoky Mountains.

Sylvain Prudhomme was born in the south of France and spent his childhood in Cameroon, Burundi, Nigeria, and Mauritius. He is the author of several books that examine contemporary Africa, and he ran the French-Senegalese Alliance in Senegal for several years. His novels include *The Great*, winner of the Prix Georges Brassens and the Prix de la Porte Dorée, and *Légende*, a finalist for the Grand Prix de l'Académie Française.

Emma Ramadan is a literary translator based in Providence, Rhode Island, where she co-owns Riffraff bookstore and bar. She is the recipient of an NEA Translation Fellowship, a PEN/Heim grant, a Fulbright scholarship, and the 2018 Albertine Prize. Her translations include *Sphinx* and *Not One Day*, by Anne Garréta, *Pretty Things*, by Virginie Despentes, *The Shutters*, by Ahmed Bouanani, and *Me & Other Writing*, by Marguerite Duras.

Leïla Slimani is the bestselling author of *The Perfect Nanny*, winner of the Prix Goncourt in 2016; *Adèle*, winner of the La Momounia Prize; and *Sex and Lies*, which examines the private lives of women in Slimani's native Morocco. A journalist and frequent commentator on women's and human rights, she serves as French president Emmanuel Macron's personal representative for the promotion of French language and culture. She lives in Paris.

Rachael Small is an editor and translator from French and Spanish, and the Director of Publicity at Europa Editions. She has an MFA in literary translation from the University of Iowa and a BA in French Studies and Creative Writing from Bard College. Her translation of Abdellah Taïa's *Another Morocco*, published by Semiotext(e), was selected as one of *World Literature Today*'s Notable Translations of 2017.

Sandra Smith is the translator of *Suite Française* and eleven other novels by Irène Némirovsky, a new translation of Camus's *L'Etranger, The Necklace and Other Stories: Maupassant for Modern Times,* and *But You Did Not Come Back,* by Marceline Loridan-Ivens, among others. She has won the PEN Translation Prize, the French-American Florence Gould Translation Prize, and the Jewish National Book Award. She currently teaches at New York University.

Helen Stevenson has translated six books by Alain Mabanckou, as well as novels by many other French writers, including Marie Darrieussecq and Alice Ferney. She has published three novels and two memoirs and lives in Somerset, UK, where she teaches piano.

Lee Stringer is the author of *Grand Central Winter, Like Shaking Hands with God,* and *Sleepaway School.* He is a two-time recipient of the Washington Irving Award and, in 2005, he received a Lannan Foundation Residency Fellowship. He is a former editor and columnist for *Street News.* His essays and articles have appeared in a variety of other publications, including the *Nation,* the *New York Times,* and *Newsday.* He lives in Mamaroneck, New York.

Sam Taylor is a novelist, translator, and journalist. He was born in England, spent eleven years in France, and now lives in the United States. His four novels have been translated into ten languages, and one of them—*The Republic of Trees*—was made into a movie. His translations from French include Laurent Binet's *The Seventh Function of Language* and Hubert Mingarelli's *Four Soldiers,* both of which were longlisted for the International Booker Prize; Maylis de Kerangal's *The Heart,* which won the French-American Translation Prize and the Lewis Galantiere Award; and Leïla Slimani's bestselling *The Perfect Nanny.*

Abdourahman Waberi is a novelist, essayist, poet, academic, and short story writer from Djibouti. He was the winner of the Grand prix littéraire d'Afrique noire in 1996 for his short story collection *Cahier nomade*. His novels include *Transit*, finalist for the Best Translated Book Award in 2013; *Passage of Tears*; and *In the United States of Africa*. He splits his time between Paris and the United States.

Alice Zeniter was born in Clamart, outside Paris, in 1986. She published her first novel, *Deux moins un égal zéro*, when she was sixteen. Her second novel was published in the United States as *Take This Man* in 2012, and she won the Prix du Livre Inter in 2013 for her novel *Sombre dimanche*. Her most recent book, *The Art of Losing*, was published in France in 2017, where it was a finalist for the Prix Goncourt, and in the United States in 2020.